The Dynamics of Writing Instruction

A Structured Process Approach for Middle and High School

PETER SMAGORINSKY
The University of Georgia

LARRY R. JOHANNESSEN
Northern Illinois University

ELIZABETH A. KAHN
James B. Conant High School, Hoffman Estates, IL

THOMAS M. McCANN
Northern Illinois University

HEINEMANN
Portsmouth, NH

Heinemann
361 Hanover Street
Portsmouth, NH 03801–3912
www.heinemann.com

Offices and agents throughout the world

The authors and publisher wish to thank those who have generously given permission to reprint borrowed material:

Portions of "From the Editor" by Louann Reid from *English Journal*, Volume 94, Number 1, September 2004. Published by the National Council of Teachers of English. Reprinted by permission of the publisher.

Excerpts from *Tall Tale America: A Legendary History of Our Humorous Heroes* by Walter Blair. Copyright © 1944, 1987 by Walter Blair. Published by the University of Chicago Press. Reprinted by permission of the publisher.

Library of Congress Cataloging-in-Publication Data
The dynamics of writing instruction : a structured process approach for middle and high school / Peter Smagorinsky ... [et al].
    p. cm.
  Includes bibliographical references and index.
  ISBN-13: 978-0-325-01193-6
  ISBN-10: 0-325-01193-1
    1. English language—Composition and exercises—Study and teaching (Middle school). 2. English language—Composition and exercises—Study and teaching (Secondary).   I. Smagorinsky, Peter.
LB1631.D97 2010
808'.0420712—dc22   2010018759

Editor: Lisa Luedeke
Development editor: Alan Huisman
Production: Vicki Kasabian
Interior and cover designs: Shawn Girsberger
Cover image: © iStockphoto.com/Umbris
Typesetter: Shawn Girsberger
Manufacturing: Steve Bernier

Printed in the United States of America on acid-free paper
14 13   VP   3 4 5

To George Hillocks, Jr.

Contents

Foreword

"N ow, use one of the highlighters for each sentence in your paragraph," the student teacher directed the eighth graders, as she distributed colored pens.

I watched as her students dutifully filled the remaining class time highlighting topic sentences in green, supporting reasons in yellow, and details in red. When the bell rang, they stuffed their vividly colored papers into their writing portfolios and went off to math or band or PE, not noticeably affected by these forty-five minutes of writing instruction.

Later, I asked the cooperating teacher and the student teacher to tell me about the activity and its purposes. It turned out they had been told in a district inservice that students would learn to organize and develop paragraphs using this method. The teachers still believed this, even though students had been taught the same activity annually, starting in fourth grade, but were clearly still struggling. The teachers also assured me that they knew that this was not the only way to organize a paragraph, and that once students mastered this method of organization, they would be encouraged to try other methods.

You may recognize their dilemma. With all the possible options of content, structure, and style, writing and teaching writing can seem chaotic. So many teachers look for an effective way to make writing instruction clear and concrete. With the best of intentions they turn to teaching a formula. Although students presumably can abandon this prescribed structure later, they rarely do once they have successfully learned it. This classroom observation reminded me of the high school writing class I had taught years earlier, where I saw the effects of this teaching dilemma firsthand.

Leaning over Kelly's shoulder as she faced the computer, I asked, "Do you need a paragraph there to show a new idea?"

"Oh no," she replied. "I don't have five sentences yet."

Honest. Kelly had learned some *rules* very well, but as a junior she was in a class for students who had not successfully mastered academic writing.

I wondered what other ideas about writing Kelly and her classmates held. I put several prompts on the board, including "What goes into a paragraph?" and "How long should it be?" Students knew that a paragraph should include the "proper words" and "a thesis, sentences, [and] details." Some of them knew that paragraphs "should be long enough for you to explain your point and describe it in full detail," while others contended that there was an acceptable length ranging from "more than one sentence" to "at least five lines" or five sentences. Those in the paragraphing-by-the-numbers camp all knew there was a right number, even though they disagreed on what it was.

These juniors and seniors knew the "rules." Yet, that knowledge had not made them writers—in their eyes or in the eyes of their teachers. For every writing task, they clung to the one formula they had learned. When the formula did not work, they questioned themselves rather than the formula. What a loss of confidence and potential!

It doesn't have to be that way. *The Dynamics of Writing Instruction* comes at just the right time for teachers who are looking for alternative approaches to writing instruction, ones that offer flexibility and possibilities rather than formulas and rules. A structured process approach does just that.

Peter, Larry, Betsy, and Tom—all experienced teachers and leaders in the profession—explain that such an approach "foregrounds process-oriented principles but also stresses the structured way in which these principles are introduced" (20). Following their guidance, teachers can readily implement this sensible, research-based approach to teaching writing. But, excellent guides that these authors are, they also stress flexibility. They most emphatically do not advocate slavishly following steps or stages or processes—theirs or anyone else's—in either writing or teaching. Instead, they offer "a blueprint of possibilities" (182) for designing a curriculum and teaching students how to write various kinds of narratives, essays, and reports.

The possibilities are both specific and adaptable. In the first chapter, teachers are invited to explore beliefs about teaching writing through a set of scenarios, turning what could be abstract into specific visions of students and learning. In Part 1, the authors also articulate the principles of a structured process approach to teaching writing. Part 2, "Theory in Practice," takes you into classrooms. You see teachers structuring curricula for six different writing tasks in which students learn the demands and expectations necessary to succeed with various kinds of writing. Each chapter also includes ways to teach language in the context of writing rather than in isolation. Part 3, "The Bigger Picture," shows how teachers might develop curricula that integrate a structured process approach.

The authors acknowledge that we face significant challenges if we are to teach in ways that help students fulfill their potential as writers. Formulaic writing and "teacher-and-text-oriented instruction" (xix) prevail in the era of high-stakes tests. A prime example of this situation was offered by a middle school principal in Illinois. Commenting on the pressure of the state tests and too much sameness in students' writing, Tracy Dell'Angela told the *Chicago Tribune*, "Even my thank-you notes read like little ISAT tests. 'I really liked having lunch with you. Here are three reasons why.'"

But I share the authors' optimism that change is possible. They ask, "Will yet another book about teaching writing make a difference?" (xvii). Yes, especially if you are part of the audience of "teachers who are dissatisfied with teaching five-paragraph themes, traditional grammar lessons, and other form-driven writing pedagogies" (xix). We will, of course, need to do the work, but the authors show us what that work looks like in the hands of teachers in actual classrooms.

For each assignment, the authors provide a task analysis, materials, and a possible sequence to support instruction, assignment sheets, and student responses to the tasks. I believe that teachers using this book can transform writing instruction because *The Dynamics of Writing Instruction* so thoroughly follows the advice of Donald Graves (1983): "Good teachers show what they mean instead of telling" (277). We urge student writers to "show not tell," but how often do we see a book written for us that *shows* us effective approaches to the teaching of writing?

I have relied on the publications of these four authors, singly and together, for most of my teaching career. They have repeatedly shown me new possibilities for teaching and learning, and I trust them. If you are ready to help students realize their full potential as writers, this is the book that will make a difference. But don't rely on my telling you so; let the authors show you how a structured process approach can transform your writing instruction.

Louann Reid
Professor of English
Colorado State University

Acknowledgments

We have many people to thank for helping this book come into being.

As our dedication suggests, we owe much to George Hillocks, our graduate school mentor, for the ideas that we elaborate in this book. The title we have chosen, *The Dynamics of Writing Instruction*, deliberately echoes the title of *The Dynamics of English Instruction, Grades 7–12* (Hillocks, McCabe, and McCampbell 1971), the book that is the foundation for much of what we know about how to teach. The fact that many decades after meeting in our graduate programs at the University of Chicago we remain close in thinking and friendship is a tribute to the community—both social and intellectual—that George provided during our MAT and PhD programs in Hyde Park.

At Heinemann, Lisa Luedeke provided leadership and support as she helped us shape the manuscript. Our friend Kristen Turner of Fordham University provided a thorough critique of a late draft that helped give the book its final form. We thank Angela Dean, who adapted the activities in Chapter 6, test-drove them in her high school classes, and provided examples of how students responded to them.

We are grateful to the school principals who invited us into their schools to work with their students: Jane Bailey, Ci)ndy Gotha, Beth Gregor, Jim Pluskota, and Diana Smith. We appreciate the teachers who worked with us to plan lessons for their students, helping us find ways to differentiate and engage all learners: Mavis Barkley, Caroline Brandt, Rebecca D'Angelo, Marianne Zerull Fried, Nancy Galas, Kelly Golubiweski, Lisa Mariani, Patricia Moll, Carrie Noland, Brandi Roderique, Laura Ryan, and Mary Kate Sennett.

Several of our colleagues have provided reliable critical assessments of our attempts to construct inquiry-based lessons to teach writing. We appreciate the insights offered by Cathy Baker, Charlotte Kulla, and Charles Sprandel. Our colleagues Connie Webber and Maria Martinez-Valiukenas helped us understand how to design lessons that accommodate the needs of English language learners. In addition, our colleagues Joyce Powell and Lisa Smith offered insight into ways to shape instruction to meet the needs of students with specific learning challenges.

Our friend Joe Flanagan evaluated how specific learning activities blended with the other language arts activities in his classes. We appreciate the steady support of our friends Ellen S. Walsh and Colleen Braun, who helped us prepare teaching materials and ready the manuscript for publication.

We cannot close without saying how much we will miss Larry Johannessen. Larry passed away at age sixty-one just as we were preparing the final version of the manuscript. Of course, his sections were ready to go; he was as dependable a person as you'll ever meet. The extended profile of Larry in the Author Biographies section covers his military and academic careers, but the list of his accomplishments cannot convey the impact Larry had on the people around him. We loved him dearly; Betsy Kahn loved him so much she was married to him for twenty-seven years. Many who spoke to us in the weeks following his death remarked about his extraordinary generosity, a trait that earned him near universal respect. Larry was a gifted teacher and writer who never hesitated to share what he had or what he knew with people who might benefit. Although RateMyProfessors.com may not provide the most authoritative account of a teacher's impact, we find the following comment worth repeating, because we have heard so many other people say something similar: "He was the best professor I have ever had! After my father I would consider him the greatest man I have ever met! His class actually changed my perspective on life!" We couldn't agree more. We hope that this, his last publication, lives up to the standard of integrity that Larry provided for us all.

Introduction

I n spite of the wealth of attention writing instruction received in the final decades of the twentieth century, the teaching of writing in middle and high schools remains, at best, uneven. National Writing Project sites have conducted countless summer institutes, and new books about teaching writing appear routinely in publishers' catalogues. Yet assessments continue to find that students' writing is less accomplished than teachers hope. Undoubtedly, the assessments themselves are not what they ought to be (Hillocks 2002). But even those with relatively good reputations, such as the National Assessment of Educational Progress, find that students in the United States are not writing as well as many people expect them to. What's going on here? And will yet another book about teaching writing make a difference?

A number of issues contribute distinctly to the problem and at the same time reinforce one another (see Smagorinsky 2010):

- Educators' experiences when they were students for the most part consisted of sitting and listening (well, sitting). Their teachers did most of the talking, and as students they were then tested on the content of the lectures or "discussions." This cycle has deep roots in Indo-European culture; Cole (2005) found evidence of a Sumerian classroom from 2,000 BCE in which the stone seats face the front, where the teacher presumably stood and talked. In recent times, research has identified *first-grade students* already so deeply acculturated to authoritarian teaching that they don't know how to respond when asked to write in open-ended ways (Smagorinsky 1999).

- In the typical large state university, teacher candidates take three years of general education and content-area courses, followed by a semester of education courses that presumably will undo sixteen-plus years of authoritarian instruction (Smagorinsky 2010).

- As part of their content-area coursework, teacher candidates take between eight and fifteen courses in departments of English. In the large state universities where most teachers get certified, this instruction often centers more on the professor's preferred approach to literary criticism than on writing pedagogy (Addington 2001; Marshall and Smith 1997). Without a strong background in writing pedagogy, teacher candidates often revert to the formulaic writing that characterized their own education and that remains widely practiced by their colleagues who are already teaching (Tremmel 2001).

- During their senior year, teacher candidates typically acquire field experience in the sorts of schools in which they themselves were educated: those stressing control-oriented pedagogies that undermine the student-centered values typically emphasized in teacher education programs.

- Teacher candidates are hired by schools whose administrators and faculty view authoritarian teaching as the norm. Because these values determine the outcome of their annual reviews, teachers often gravitate to authoritarian instruction, perpetuating the cycle (Zeichner and Tabachnik 1981).

- External mandates in the form of district, state, and national standards and exams reinforce the notion that authoritarian instruction is the natural state of teaching and learning and that "teaching to the test" is the best way to produce results that make administrators and taxpayers happy.

One principal who was interviewing candidates for a teaching position made a typical remark after a newly certified applicant critiqued traditional grammar instruction and described alternatives: "Well now, I know that they tell you that stuff up there. But y'all are *down here* now." "Down here" is where the definition of quality teaching is established when it comes to hiring and retention; little value is given to the ideas from "up there" in the rarified air of the university.

The cycle of being apprenticed to teacher-and-text-oriented instruction for roughly fifteen years, being briefly exposed to alternatives, and then returning to schools where authoritarian values determine what counts as effective teaching has proven very difficult to break. Although Applebee (1974) identifies other traditions that have infiltrated schools, generally under the umbrella of "student-centered" approaches, the most prevalent form of instruction continues to locate authority in teachers and texts rather than in students. This approach to teaching has been roundly critiqued in colleges of education (Applebee 1993, 1996; Cuban 1993; and many others), by the relatively small percentage of teachers who are members of the National Council of Teachers of English and other professional organizations, and by legions of students who regard school as a prison. Yet it remains the norm, no doubt for reasons that follow from the cycle of authoritarian schooling we have outlined.

Call us crazy, but we have written this book in the hope that it will offer alternatives to teachers who are dissatisfied with teaching five-paragraph themes, traditional grammar lessons, and other form-driven writing pedagogies. Frankly, we don't expect to convert schools wholesale to our way of thinking with this effort. We do hope, however, to add to the body of work that details ways to teach writing that attend to learning processes through task-related student activity.

This volume falls within a teaching tradition that is relatively new to the Heinemann catalogue. This approach—which we refer to as a *structured process*—was developed by George Hillocks during his years as a middle school English teacher in Euclid, Ohio, during the 1960s (Hillocks 2005). Through this method he and his colleagues taught with great effectiveness in Euclid schools, under the auspices of the Project English Demonstration Center (see Hillocks et al. 1971; Hillocks and McCampbell 1965). In addition to this pedagogical success, Hillocks and his students have researched this method and found it highly effective (e.g., Hillocks et al. 1983; Lee 1993; Smagorinsky 1991a; Smith 1989). In a more comprehensive research review, Hillocks (1986a) found that over a twenty-year period, structured process writing instruction provided greater gains for student writers than did any other method of teaching writing.

Briefly, the Hillocksian tradition is founded on the idea that kids learn well when actively engaged with things that interest them. Learning begins with activity rather than with the abstract presentations of information that typify much school instruction. Teachers design and sequence activities that allow students to move through increasingly challenging problems of the same type. Their learning is highly social, involving continual talk with one another as they learn procedures and strategies for undertaking tasks.

Although the teacher might identify the task (e.g., writing an argument) and design activities that enable students to take on increasingly complex problems (e.g., moving from arguing which compact disc cover is most appealing to arguing which social group in school has the greatest influence to arguing whether or not technology contributes to or detracts from human progress), most of the talking and doing comes from the students.

We should say up front that we see merit in other ways of teaching writing. We do not argue that we have discovered the one best way to teach writing; rather, we want to stimulate your thinking by reviewing in detail one way we all found successful in a variety of high schools. If you find that this method works with your students, we encourage you to think about how to apply the principles to other writing demands in your curriculum.

How This Book Is Organized

We begin inductively. In the first chapter, we ask you to think about possible ways of teaching writing in middle and high schools. Then we suggest that you think about your assumptions about teaching writing, where they came from, and what types of instruction they produce. After you have considered our scenarios depicting a range of approaches to teaching writing, we ask you to position your own beliefs in relation to them and write a scenario that portrays your own approach to writing instruction. In the second chapter we outline the structured process approach to teaching writing, a method that follows from what we learned from working with Hillocks and how we applied those principles in our own teaching.

The second part of the book consists of six chapters that apply this instructional approach to types of writing commonly taught in middle and secondary schools: personal narratives, fictional narratives, essays of argumentation, comparison and contrast essays, extended definition essays, and research reports. In these chapters we outline what a structured process approach looks like in a classroom and explain our thinking about how we designed the activities.

The final part of the book, Chapter 9, outlines a comprehensive writing curriculum in which teachers might use structured process instruction to teach students a range of processes for engaging in different types of tasks in relation to different areas of the curriculum. This curriculum outline suggests one possible way to think about writing instruction in the long and broad term, not a rigid scope and sequence unresponsive to local conditions.

Our approach is designed to work in dialogue with your teaching, first through the consideration of teaching possibilities and ultimately through our effort to illustrate a type of design process that we apply to commonly taught writing tasks, and that we hope teachers can then adapt to other types of writing. Ultimately, readers are invited to create their own instruction in response to the challenges that they find in their schools and districts, in the needs of their students, and in the demands of writing opportunities that help students grow into more reflective thinkers, writers, and people.

PART

I

A Framework for Teaching Writing

Approaches to Teaching Writing

I f you hope to teach a classroom of middle school or high school students to write, where do you start? You have many options from which to select or shape your writing instruction, and each approach assumes much about the nature of writing, the process of learning, and the effects of teaching on writing development. Questioning these assumptions allows you to teach well in relation to what students need. (If you don't question the assumptions behind the instructional approaches you use, it might not matter how you teach!)

By considering several approaches to teaching writing and talking about them with colleagues, you can make explicit the beliefs and understandings that guide your development of lesson plans, the way you teach those plans, the adjustments you make from episode to episode within a lesson, and your reflection on the effects of your instruction when all is said and done.

A traditional approach to developing a theory of instruction would likely begin with reviewing the related literature to see what other thinkers have had to say about writing and the teaching of writing. Another, more inductive, approach is to think about teaching from the ground up, starting with the classroom, developing a theory by considering practice. In this chapter we take this second approach, inviting you to think about your beliefs about teaching as a way to open a conversation about how to teach writing.

Eight Approaches to Teaching Others to Write

We have developed eight scenarios that reveal the thinking behind the instructional strategies teachers use to teach writing. These snapshots represent actual practices that have been defended and championed in publications and presentations, but they do not re-create the rich complexity of instructional context; particular approaches offer the most promise in particular contexts. As you read the descriptions, judge the value of each approach relative to the others as well as to your own experiences as a student and teacher. You may readily embrace some of these approaches; others will not resonate as much; some may have no appeal at all. You need to judge for yourself, perhaps in conjunction with colleagues and others interested in writing instruction, which approach or combination of approaches offers the best possibility of helping your student writers fulfill their promise.

As you read, take mental or written notes that will help you consider the possibilities and problems of each approach and reflect on each in relation to the others. How do you see yourself, your students, your school, and your community in these scenarios, and what potentials do they reveal that might provoke change in your beliefs about effective teaching? What ideas do you find ill advised and what troubles you about them? Where do you see your teaching headed over the course of your career, and how does thinking about these scenarios help you clarify your understanding of how to get there?

Scenario 1: Stressing the Classic Form

Ken Greenway has been assigned to teach an eleventh-/twelfth-grade class called "Writing for College" and is uncertain how to go about it. Drawing on his own past experience as a learner, he recalls how he learned to write essays when he was a freshman at Middle Border State University. Although Ken found the instruction of the graduate teaching assistant helpful, he especially relied on a book by Sidney Moss called *Composition by Logic*, which he found in a bin of used books at the college bookstore. Using this book as his guide, Ken trains his own students to write carefully organized five-paragraph essays focused around a "three-part analytic thesis sentence," a structure Ken feels neophyte writers can readily understand.

After six weeks, Ken is delighted when the compositions his students turn in feature a three-part thesis sentence, body paragraphs that develop each of the three parts, and a fifth and concluding paragraph in which the writer sums up the major points. Ken shares this promising development with his department chair, and she congratulates him for training students to write in a way that is consistent with the scoring standard on the state writing assessment.

Scenario 2: Individualizing Instruction

Murray Daniels worries that the dominant practices in schools strip students of their natural, authentic voices and train them to function as automatons spouting school-sponsored and state-sponsored artificial language. Murray works against the tide by encouraging students to write, write, write, following their own inclinations to discuss whatever they want, in whatever form appeals to them. His one unyielding demand is that students continue to write. A glimpse into Murray's classroom finds students at work in their journals or writing poems, scripts, stories, reflections, lists, vignettes, letters, the beginnings of projected novels, and other kinds of text. Murray often plays soft music as the students write.

Murray usually writes along with his students, and he holds regular conferences in which he helps students clarify and develop their plans and find their voice. When Murray meets with students one-on-one, he tries not to direct them, since he feels that would be taking ownership of their work; instead, he asks questions to help students discover their own intents and gain confidence in their own choices as writers. The students' composing processes include exploring and discovering, planning, composing, conferring, revising, editing, and publishing. He encourages them to mix conventions from their colloquial voices and online writing (the acronyms used in text messages, for example) with "standard" conventions as long as they serve a legitimate purpose. He occasionally shares his own writing with his students and encourages them to share their writing with the rest of the class.

Murray assesses his students' growth and their progress toward achieving their personal writing goals by examining their journals and portfolios and (with some discomfort) assigning grades. The students' portfolios are a record of their writing and reveal their growth as writers over time.

Scenario 3: Learning from Accomplished Writers

Stella Mulligan works tirelessly to teach her students to write. Her inventive writing assignments identify a particular audience, specify a purpose for the composition, and reveal the assessment criteria, such as, "Imagine that you are writing to a time traveler from the nineteenth century who is about to enroll at this high school. Explain what he/she needs to know to be able to function safely and successfully in this new environment. The quality of your essay will be judged by the appropriate match between diction and audience, the logical organization of the discussion, and the thoroughness of the development."

Stella typically leads classroom examinations of exemplary writing of the kind she wants her students to produce. Sometimes these models are the work of published authors; sometimes they are the work of other students who have given her permission to use their compositions for this purpose.

She believes her inventive assignments inspire her students to want to write and that the models she presents show students what the writing should look like. When students turn in their work, Stella reads each effort carefully, edits it to show where the student has erred, and writes extensive comments explaining the nature of the errors and telling the writer how his or her work can be improved. These written comments and corrections constitute the bulk of her writing instruction.

Scenario 4: Studying the Sentence

When the bell rings, Thad Townsend tells his eleventh graders to open their *English Grammar and Composition* textbook to the beginning of the chapter on restrictive and nonrestrictive elements. As the students follow along, Thad reads aloud the descriptions of restrictive and nonrestrictive elements. He then asks his students to begin the exercises at the end of the chapter on punctuating restrictive and nonrestrictive sentence elements correctly. They will later complete these exercises as homework.

Next, Thad writes a complicated sentence on the board and asks a student, at random, to describe each element in the sentence in grammatical terms: the part of speech, its function in the sentence (e.g., appositive, objective complement, auxiliary, etc.), the mood of the verb, the case of the pronoun, and the reason for the punctuation. This activity is part of Thad's program for helping students develop a formal vocabulary that will allow them to conduct an interior dialogue about the writing they are producing or revising and discuss that writing with others.

Thad values precise language and knows his insistence on correct usage and grammar will pay off with strong scores on his students' college board exams. Based on his own education, he believes grammar and usage exercises foster language skills that will transfer to students' everyday speech and written essays. Even though the improvement may not be immediately apparent, the effect, he is confident, will be cumulative. The full impact of his teaching may not be evident until long after his students have taken his class.

Scenario 5: Understanding Syntactic Choices

Gwen Royster's writing instruction consists of a series of activities in which students analyze sentences and paragraphs written by contemporary authors and then produce their own sentences and paragraphs. She frequently assigns sentence-combining activities in which students write the "base clause" in uncomplicated active voice and provide rich details via "free modifiers," especially appositives, prepositional phrases, absolutes, and relative clauses. Gwen then leads discussions about the relative merits and the effects of the sentence elements the students have combined. She often demonstrates "sentence notation" on a video monitor, showing students that each sentence has *levels of modification*, *direction of movement*, and *texture*. She follows similar practices to show the structure of paragraphs. Gwen feels that by understanding the structures of sentences and paragraphs and the generative nature of their construction, students are able to take command of their own efforts to compose.

Scenario 6: Beginning with Activity

Before Betsy Jo Hansen has her eighth graders write narratives, she takes them through a series of preparatory activities. After telling her students that they will be writing a story that has many of the features of the stories they will be reading and discussing in class, she darkens the classroom and projects a picture of a dark, deserted alley. In the photo, a distant light casts eerie shadows across the pavement and highlights the contrast between wet ground and dark puddles. Several gritty dumpsters are lined up against the buildings on the right of the photo.

Betsy Jo prompts each student to imagine that she or he is alone, crouched between two of the dumpsters, hearing the footfalls of someone approaching. She plays a recording of footsteps on wet pavement, growing louder and more distinct. Working individually, the students jot down other sounds they might hear in the alley, the smells around them, and the emotions they might experience.

Then, in groups of three, they discuss who the approaching stranger might be: a homicidal maniac stalking a victim, a dreaded enemy seeking revenge, a law officer searching for an escapee, a mobster seeking to bump off a rival, a passerby looking for a place to discard a sandwich wrapper. Students suggest possibilities and their partners agree or disagree, suggest variations and details, or question the scenario's feasibility.

Next each student drafts a story, paying special attention to details that will bring the situation and setting to life. Anticipating that her students will need help with some of the mechanics, Betsy Jo models developing and punctuating dialogue. The students then exchange drafts with a partner, edit them, and recommend revisions based on what they need to know as readers. After two more drafts based on further peer response, the students publish their stories in a class collection.

Scenario 7: Producing Multigenre Texts

Phineas Talbot introduces his seventh graders to a multigenre approach to writing. In connection with reading Melba Patillo Beals' memoir (1995) of the 1957 integration of Central High School in Little Rock, Arkansas, *Warriors Don't Cry*, students put together a variety of texts to create a facsimile of the

~~high school's yearbook from that year.~~ Phineas provides extensive written instructions, along with descriptions of possible elements to include: photo montages depicting high school life in 1957; feature stories about the notable events of the year; high school seniors' predictions and hopes for the future for themselves, their community, and the nation; profiles of exceptional teachers and administrators; and poems that distill the drama and emotion of the school year.

Phineas is impressed with the variety and creativity of the work the students complete. They have discovered a repertoire of ways to compose in several genres. Some students even create additional audio- or videotapes capturing memorable episodes in the lives of certain students at the school. Since Phineas has no examples from previous classes and there are no conventional standards for assessing such assignments, he is generous in his grading, crediting students with meeting the basic requirements outlined in their written directions.

Scenario 8: Inquiring into Local Concerns

Hammond Bienz teaches in an urban school. Like many first-year teachers, he has been assigned low-level classes in his school's tracking system, and his students are resistant to the grammar books he uses to teach writing at the beginning of the year.

After weeks of endless battles, Hamm is desperate for something that will interest them. He brings in copies of the city newspaper, and the class discusses what news was considered worthy of inclusion and what news was not reported. The students discover that their own neighborhoods are not represented—there are no stories about youth centers, local singers and musicians, hobbies and pastimes of local residents, facets of youth culture, efforts of local business owners, actions of law-abiding citizens to improve community life, and other things of interest to them.

Hamm makes learning about and reporting on the local community the focus of the class. As homework, students interview people, record local performers, take photographs and videos, and otherwise document community life. Class time is spent talking about how to present their findings on a website in as appealing a way as possible (including using colloquial language). These "remedial" students create a website that gets more hits than the official school website, and each student receives an A for the class.

Thinking About Your Own Beliefs

These eight scenarios represent a range of beliefs about the nature of writing, the respective roles of students and teachers, the degree to which writing conventions are fixed or flexible, freedom versus control in teaching and learning, and much else. Use the matrix in Figure 1–1 to codify your position on the following "tensions":

1. *Freedom vs. control.* The scenarios range from teachers who tightly control writing instruction (e.g., focusing on correct sentence formation) to those who yield considerable authority to students (e.g., basing instruction on student inquiries into what interests them). Where do you stand on this continuum between freedom and control? Which scenario best represents your position?

2. *Student activity vs. student receptivity.* The scenarios portray instruction in which students are highly active (e.g., beginning with activity and attending to rules later) or highly receptive (e.g., producing the forms specified by teachers). Where do you stand on this continuum between activity and receptivity? Which scenario best represents your position?

3. *Existing conventions vs. student-generated conventions.* The scenarios reflect different attitudes toward conventions, with some teachers stressing the use of textbook conventions (e.g., following given forms for grammar and paragraph structure) and others allowing students to determine the appropriateness of the conventions they employ (e.g., allowing text messaging acronyms in student writing). Where do you stand on this continuum between existing and student-generated conventions? Which scenario best represents your position?

4. *Structured instruction vs. free-flowing instruction.* The scenarios depict teachers structuring their teaching quite differently, from those whose instruction is highly structured (e.g., going systematically through a series of steps or concepts) to those who allow students to define their own goals and trajectories (e.g., using a "workshop" approach in which students go off in personal directions). Where do you stand on this continuum between structured and free-flowing instruction? Which scenario best represents your position?

5. *Exclusive attention to written language vs. attention to other modes of expression.* In the scenarios some teachers consider writing only in the alphabetic sense (e.g., stressing the production of five-paragraph themes) while others allow students to mix writing with other media (e.g., encouraging multigenre composing). Where do you stand on this continuum between written and multimodal conceptions of composition? Which scenario best represents your position?

Figure 1–1. Your Position in Relation to the Scenarios and Tensions

Align yourself with each scenario in relation to each tension. In the box where each scenario and tension intersect, jot notes that may help you think about where you stand or where you'd like to be in your teaching. You may want to compare notes with one or more colleagues and talk about your areas of agreement and disagreement.

	Freedom vs. Control	Student Activity vs. Student Receptivity	Existing Conventions vs. Student-Generated Conventions	Structured Instruction vs. Free-Flowing Instruction	Exclusive Attention to Written Language vs. Attention to Other Modes of Expression	Imitating Qualities of Accomplished Writers vs. Generating New Forms Based on Students' Needs and Concerns
Scenario 1 *Stressing the Classic Form*						
Scenario 2 *Individualizing Instruction*						
Scenario 3 *Learning from Accomplished Writers*						
Scenario 4 *Studying the Sentence*						

	Freedom vs. Control	Student Activity vs. Student Receptivity	Existing Conventions vs. Student-Generated Conventions	Structured Instruction vs. Free-Flowing Instruction	Exclusive Attention to Written Language vs. Attention to Other Modes of Expression	Imitating Qualities of Accomplished Writers vs. Generating New Forms Based on Students' Needs and Concerns
Scenario 5 *Understanding Syntactic Choices*						
Scenario 6 *Beginning with Activity*						
Scenario 7 *Producing Multigenre Texts*						
Scenario 8 *Inquiring into Local Concerns*						

(continues)

Figure 1–1. Your Position in Relation to the Scenarios and Tensions (*continued*)

	Teacher as the Primary Evaluative Audience vs. Other Readers Who Might Evaluate	Preparing Students for College vs. Teaching Writing Irrespective of College Demands	Teaching Students vs. Teaching the Subject	Writing as an Exclusive Focus vs. Writing as Part of an Integrated Curriculum	Student Interaction Around Their Writing vs. Student Isolation to Produce Independent Work	A Focus on Product vs. a Focus on Process
Scenario 1 *Stressing the Classic Form*						
Scenario 2 *Individualizing Instruction*						
Scenario 3 *Learning from Accomplished Writers*						
Scenario 4 *Studying the Sentence*						

	Teacher as the Primary Evaluative Audience vs. Other Readers Who Might Evaluate	Preparing Students for College vs. Teaching Writing Irrespective of College Demands	Teaching Students vs. Teaching the Subject	Writing as an Exclusive Focus vs. Writing as Part of an Integrated Curriculum	Student Interaction Around Their Writing vs. Student Isolation to Produce Independent Work	A Focus on Product vs. a Focus on Process
Scenario 5 *Understanding Syntactic Choices*						
Scenario 6 *Beginning with Activity*						
Scenario 7 *Producing Multigenre Texts*						
Scenario 8 *Inquiring into Local Concerns*						

6. ~~Imitating qualities of accomplished writers vs. generating new forms based~~ *on students' needs and concerns.* Some scenarios reveal teachers who stress the imitation of published writers or the production of given forms (e.g., reading model essays prior to writing) while others show teachers who value students' development of their own forms (e.g., creating web-based texts in order to publish their work). Where do you stand on this continuum between imitating model writers and generating new forms of representation? Which scenario best represents your position?

7. *The teacher as the primary evaluative audience vs. other readers (e.g., peer groups or people outside class) who might evaluate student compositions.* The scenarios include teachers who personally collect and grade all student writing (e.g., using feedback on papers as a primary means of instruction) and those who present student work to broader audiences in order to confirm its quality (e.g., posting student work to a website). Where do you stand on this continuum between teachers and other audiences as arbiters of the quality of student composition? Which scenario best represents your position?

8. *Preparing students for college vs. teaching writing irrespective of college demands.* The teachers in the scenarios take different approaches to their instruction relative to college preparation, ranging from focusing on college preparation (e.g., explicitly aiming instruction toward presumed college standards) to focusing on learners' more immediate needs (e.g., basing instruction on their present interests). Where do you stand on this continuum between college preparation and immediate needs? Which scenario best represents your position?

9. *Teaching students vs. teaching the subject.* Some teachers in the scenarios disregard the curriculum in order to allow students to create their own topics and standards (e.g., enabling students to do community research and present it using local speech customs) while others emphasize the content of the discipline of English as established through the centuries (e.g., adhering to the precepts of grammarians and their textbooks). Where do you stand on this continuum between teaching students and teaching the subject? Which scenario best represents your position?

10. *Writing as an exclusive focus vs. writing as part of an integrated curriculum.* The scenarios reflect different views of the place of writing in the curriculum, ranging from writing as a distinct activity (e.g., taught in "writing workshops" or through discrete lessons in language usage) to writing as integrated with the language and literature

(and perhaps other) strands of the curriculum (e.g., as part of a multigenre unit built around a common class literary reading). Where do you stand on this continuum between teaching writing as a separate focus and teaching writing in conjunction with other curricular strands? Which scenario best represents your position?

11. *Student interaction around their writing vs. student isolation to produce independent work.* In the scenarios some teachers provide students opportunities to talk about their writing before, while, and after they draft their texts (e.g., having students discuss ideas and respond to drafts of their stories based on a projected image of a deserted alley) while others view assistance as a version of cheating and discourage it (e.g., instructing students in composition form without providing class time for students to discuss their work with one another). Where do you stand on this continuum between allowing students to discuss their writing throughout the process and discouraging any student interaction because it compromises the integrity of individual performance? Which scenario best represents your position?

12. *A focus on product vs. a focus on process.* The scenarios depict teachers focusing on the finished product of student writing (e.g., emphasizing form by providing model essays) and focusing on the processes that students go through to arrive at a product (e.g., using sentence-combining exercises that help students develop strategies for varying their syntactic structures). Where do you stand on this continuum between emphasizing product or process? Which scenario best represents your position?

Writing Your Own Scenario

Jerome Bruner (1986) proposes that thinking may be accomplished in two ways. The most common academic mode is what he calls *paradigmatic* thinking, which includes logical and scientific thought that "makes use of procedures to assure verifiable reference and to test for empirical truth" (13). The outline of a theory is one common form of paradigmatic thought, typically relying on scholarly sources, conventional forms of argumentation, and logical means of persuasion.

Narrative thought, in contrast, "strives to put . . . timeless miracles into the particulars of experience, and to locate the experience in time and place" (Bruner 1986, 13). The narrative mode has the potential to embody a theory of writing instruction without the scholarly congestion that, many find, obscures their reading of formal, paradigmatic presentations of writing theory. Bruner has described the role of the arts, including narrative, this way:

It has been the convention of most schools to treat the arts of narrative—song, drama, fiction, theater, whatever—as more "decoration" than necessity. . . . Despite that, we frame the accounts of our cultural origins and our most cherished beliefs in story form, and it is not just the "content" of these stories that grips us, but their narrative artifice. (1996, 40)

We agree that narratives provide more than ornamentation and that they may potentially embody just as robust a conception of teaching or other cultural activity as the most rigorous of arguments.

Now that you've considered these scenarios and the tensions they present, and thought about your own beliefs in light of them, *write a scenario depicting yourself as a writing teacher.*

Since your scenario is meant to embody a theory of writing, focus on depicting yourself as a teacher whose instruction is consistent and coherent; that is, you would not allow free-form writing and then micro-correct students' use of grammar. You might also describe the teacher you hope to become rather than the teacher you are at the moment. Feel free to combine elements from any of the scenarios we've presented or include aspects of writing instruction we've overlooked in our scenarios. Also, note that we condensed our scenarios for purposes of illustration. You are welcome to extend yours in whatever detail you feel is necessary in order to portray your conception of writing instruction.

Considering the Sources of Your Beliefs

Where did your conception of writing instruction, as evidenced in your scenario, come from? Most of us do not develop beliefs out of thin air but rather draw on preexisting ideas and experiences. Use the following questions to uncover the origins of your present beliefs:

1. How have your own experiences as a student in classes where writing was assigned—both in English classes and in other disciplines—influenced your thinking about how to teach writing?

2. How have your experiences with writing outside school contributed to your beliefs about the effective teaching of writing in school?

3. How have your experiences in and out of school with other tools (music, art, etc.) affected your beliefs about how to teach writing?

4. How have your experiences as a teacher affected your understanding of how to teach writing?

5. Which scholarly sources (educational theorists, composition authorities, professors, etc.) have most influenced your thinking about how to teach writing, and what has been their influence?

6. What other writers (e.g., language columnists, stylebook writers, authors who have written about their writing, colleagues and friends who write) have influenced your beliefs about how to teach writing?

7. In what ways have policy statements and curriculum mandates affected your personal theory of writing instruction?

8. What has been the role of "shoptalk" with colleagues—either in your own school or at professional meetings—in the development of your beliefs about writing pedagogy?

9. How have your own students influenced your beliefs about how to teach writing?

Of these experiences, which do you draw on to inform your decisions about how to teach writing? Do you trust some sources more than others? Why do some sources make better sense to you than others? On the whole, how have these sources helped you to generate for yourself a theory about how to teach writing?

At this point (or after you've finished reading this book), revisit your scenario. Has your thinking about appropriate writing instruction changed or been enriched as a result of your archeological dig into your experiences as a student and teacher? How might you modify your scenario to account for these new considerations?

Another possibility is to generate a series of simple "I believe . . ." statements that you periodically reflect on and revise as your thinking about teaching writing evolves and that could eventually contribute to a more paradigmatic presentation of your philosophy of teaching writing. However you take on this task, use this opportunity to lay out your beliefs about how to teach writing, and consider how you came to develop them.

Questions for Reflection

After reacting to the scenarios in this chapter, consulting with several critical friends, and reflecting on your judgments about the elements that would comprise a viable approach to the teaching of writing, you should be able to compose an extended statement that represents your vision. Here are a few considerations to guide your thinking and expression:

1. *Characteristics of the Learners*: What are the characteristics of the learners whom you imagine you will be teaching? For example, are they beginning middle school, or leaving high school? Are they from affluent communities or from areas challenged by poverty? Are the learners new arrivals to the United States, long-term language

learners, or native speakers of a dominant dialect of English? Why would it matter who the learners are? Do all learners learn in more or less the same way?

2. *The Nature of Writing*: What is the nature of writing? Perhaps your answer will depend on the kind of writing you envision your students composing, or perhaps you imagine all writing tasks to be essentially the same. How would this understanding of the nature of the act and processes of writing guide your decisions about the most appropriate instructional activities?

3. *Instructional Activities*: What do you imagine as the key instructional activities that will promote growth in writing proficiency? For example, is it important to examine models of quality writing? Is it important to have a variety of writing experiences? Should students engage in drills in usage, punctuation, and spelling? Do you imagine students engaged in problem-solving activities? Would learners write often in journals? Would learners select topics and formats of their own choosing, or would they complete teacher-sponsored assignments? What sequence would the writers follow? What reasons do you have to support the use of any of the activities?

4. *Oral Discourse*: How important is oral discourse as an element in a writing process? Do you place much importance in conferences between instructor and learner? Do you value peer review as a stage in a composing process? Can you imagine students engaged in small-group and large-group discussions as essential elements in the preparation for writing? In the end, why would any of these interactions be important?

5. *Learning Environment*: What would you emphasize as the characteristics of the learning environment? Would writing instruction be embedded in integrated units of instruction that are rich with reading, discussing, listening, and viewing? To what extent would you depend on instructional technologies to support teaching and learning? What would be the necessary feeling tone in the class, and why is this a consideration?

6. *Assessment*: What part does assessment play in supporting the learning to write? If you assume that assessment is an important instructional element, what form should assessment take, and why?

A Structured Process Approach to Teaching Writing

L ike you, we have, throughout our teaching careers, encountered many different beliefs about how to teach writing. We've walked many miles in many pairs of shoes, experimenting with any number of provocative approaches. Nevertheless, our foundation, not just for teaching writing but for whatever we teach, remains the approach we learned while working with George Hillocks at the University of Chicago. Hillocks' principles rest on two key ideas: *environmental teaching* and *inquiry instruction*.

In an environmental approach, teachers design materials and activities in which students develop thinking processes and strategies in relation to particular tasks. A task in this sense is both intellectual and practical: it involves both *doing* something and *thinking about how it's done* so that it can be done again with different materials. Examples of these kinds of tasks include comparing and contrasting similar yet different things, arguing in favor of a solution, and defining an abstract term (such as *cruelty to animals* or *clean air*). An important assumption is that the task involves unique ways of thinking—for example, defining *effective leadership* and writing a narrative about an effective leader illustrate the qualities of leadership in different ways. A key feature of an environmental approach, then, is that one learns different procedures for accomplishing different tasks.

Environmental teaching is also embedded in real experiences. For example, to learn comparison and contrast strategies, students might study menus from different restaurants in order to choose a site for an anniversary party. Or they might use a set of real or fictional scenarios depicting people's actions in order to generate criteria for concepts such as *progress*, *maturity*, or *loyalty*.

An environmental approach brings "teacher, students, and materials into balance" (Hillocks 1986a, 247). The teacher designs appropriate task-based activities, and the students use these materials as the medium of engagement. The teacher helps students develop goal-directed thinking rather than telling them what to think. Students inductively generate appropriate processes and strategies for achieving a goal—writing an extended definition, producing a convincing argument, and so on. Their imagination is cultivated along with their strategic thinking. In this approach, *task* does not have the negative connotations often associated with the term.

Instruction focusing on inquiry presumes that students, working in collaboration, will manipulate "data sets" (materials) in order to generate and organize ideas, analyze data, and anticipate and respond to different points of view. The activities may have several plausible solutions or outcomes.

Hillocks' *environmental* label never caught on, perhaps because it seems more ecological than pedagogical, and *inquiry* is now applied to virtually any student-oriented instruction. We therefore prefer Arthur Applebee's (1986) term *structured process*, which foregrounds process-oriented principles but also stresses the structured way in which these principles are introduced.

General Principles

The following principles are characteristic of the structured process approach to teaching writing. Also see Figure 2–1 for an abbreviated "highlights" version.

1. Instruction allows students to develop composition procedures in relation to particular tasks, such as argumentation, description, narration, extended definition, fable, or any other specific type of writing that relies on particular social and rhetorical conventions. For instance, to compose a formal argument, writers need to know how to generate claims, evidence, warrants, potential responses, and rebuttals. Such task-specific knowledge is not necessary for writing a fable, a sonnet, a narrative, or many other types of writing.

2. Because different tasks require different procedures, writing instruction cannot rely solely on generally useful strategies (freewriting, drafting, etc.), even though these strategies can be

incorporated. There is therefore no general "writing process." Rather, there are many writing processes, and skillful writers know how to vary their procedures for writing to suit the situation and the task (Schneider 2003).

3. When writing instruction focuses on specific tasks, students work toward clear and specific goals with a particular community of readers in mind. These readers' expectations for the presentation and expression of the writer's ideas determine quality; the writing itself

Figure 2–1. Compendium of Principles of Structured Process Instruction

1. Students develop composition procedures in relation to particular tasks.

2. Writing instruction cannot rely solely on generally useful strategies.

3. Students work toward clear and specific goals with particular readers in mind.

4. Thinking and writing are open-ended.

5. Composing is a highly social act.

6. Teachers identify the criteria needed to assess writing in given genres for given readerships.

7. Teachers orchestrate student activity.

8. Teachers scaffold students' learning by designing activities and providing manipulative materials.

9. Students learn procedures through accessible tasks and apply them to more intricate tasks of the same type.

10. Student activity, often in small groups, is essential.

11. Students share their work frequently.

12. When possible, the teacher provides additional readerships for students' writing.

13. People learn to write by talking, as well as by writing.

14. Models are minimized or discarded. Attention to form comes later.

15. Modeling of thinking processes may be appropriate.

16. Assessments allow students to apply learned procedures to new tasks.

has no inherent qualities. That is, to paraphrase Nystrand (1986), good writing is *in tune* with the conventions, discourse, syntax, and other expectations of its intended readers.

4. Even with clear and specific goals, thinking and writing are open-ended; writers need to construct new ideas and meaning in order to write effectively in relation to their readers' expectations.

5. Given the relational nature of writing that follows from Nystrand's premise, composing is a highly social act, rather than the work of an isolated individual. The social nature of writing is evident in the ways in which writers must know their readers, the ways in which conventions link writers to the history of writing, and the ways in which writing instruction can incorporate considerable peer interaction at most stages of the students' writing process.

6. In considering the expectations of a community of readers, teachers should identify the criteria needed to assess the strengths and weaknesses of writing in given genres for given readerships. By identifying these qualities, teachers are telling themselves what they need to teach students how to do in order to produce writing that is in tune with their readers' expectations. Further, they are informing students of the criteria by which they will be assessed, and of the distinctions that will differentiate one grade from another when their writing is evaluated. In many instances, teachers and learners derive the criteria together by examining a set of sample compositions and discussing their relative merits.

7. The teacher's role is to orchestrate student activity rather than lecture (on the one extreme) or leave students to their own devices (on the other extreme). Taking a structured process approach, teachers typically do a lot of work outside class, while students do a lot of work in class. In other words, the teacher spends considerable time outside class designing activities that will engage learners in writing processes; during class, the students participate in these activities under the teacher's guidance.

8. Teachers scaffold students' learning by designing activities and providing materials (Hillocks 1995). The materials are manipulative—that is, they may be handled (both materially and mentally), rearranged, reconstituted, reinterpreted, and otherwise moved about during the process of discussion and composition to facilitate students' thinking about the problems they are solving.

9. As part of students' scaffolded activity, they move from more accessible tasks to more intricate tasks, employing the procedures developed during the initial stages of instruction to both frame and solve increasingly complex problems of a similar type.

10. Student activity, often in small groups, is an essential stage of their inductive, collaborative development of strategies for meeting the expectations of particular tasks. Rather than being told what their writing process should be, students participate in activities that enable them to develop appropriate procedures for accomplishing the task. High levels of peer interaction are the medium through which students learn procedures to guide their manipulation of content in the execution of particular tasks.

11. While the teacher often serves as the primary evaluative audience for student writing, students share their work frequently as they write and get feedback from their peers. This feedback assists the writer, who incorporates the feedback into revisions. It also benefits the critic, who gets exposure to other writers working on the same problem and develops critical skills by considering how others' writing might be improved.

12. When possible, teachers provide additional readerships for students' writing, such as having students send their arguments about local policy issues to key stakeholders, enter their writing in competitions, send letters and other writing to newspapers, post their writing on the Internet, and otherwise use their writing for authentic communicative purposes.

13. The emphasis on student interaction at most stages of their writing process requires a revision of conventional wisdom about writing. Many writing authorities claim that people learn to write by writing. From the perspective we outline in this book, students learn to write by talking, as well as by writing, an insight we have learned through conversations with our friend and colleague Michael W. Smith.

14. Models for students to follow in their writing are minimized or discarded. The emphasis in this approach is on developing procedures for rendering ideas into text, rather than beginning with form and assuming that students will have ideas to plug into the form. While form ultimately matters, it comes later in the process. The students' ideas and their need to express and communicate them provide the impetus for this approach to writing instruction.

15. Teachers may nevertheless *model a process* for thinking about a problem. This modeling might take the form of thinking aloud while engaging in the task, orchestrating group composing as students learn a new set of procedures, or other ways of revealing how to think while working.

16. Assessments are geared toward students' application of procedural knowledge to new tasks. Typically, in school, students are evaluated on their ability to recall information from prior reading, lectures, and discussions. A structured process approach liberates students from dependence on the teacher by emphasizing procedures that may be used in future actions. Assessment, then, allows students to apply the learned procedures to a new task.

Task and Activity Analysis

Designing and sequencing activities that will guide students through a process for writing in accordance with the demands of a given task requires two types of analysis. In a *task analysis*, we consider what is involved in completing a given task—what is involved in writing a personal narrative, in writing a fable, in writing a satire, and so on. In an *activity analysis*, we consider what materials and related activities will enable students to develop procedures for engaging with similar sorts of tasks in the future. We engage in task and activity analyses in the initial stages of planning as a way to set our goals, and continually revisit them during the design process to make sure that our instruction is aligned with the purpose of instruction.

Task Analysis

1. Goals, objectives, or outcomes:

   * What is the purpose of the instruction?

   * What kinds of final products will the students be responsible for?

   * What intermediate processes and products will be involved as students work their way toward a final product?

2. Knowledge needed to perform the task:

   * What kinds of things does a student need to know in order to accomplish tasks of this type?

   * Is content knowledge required?

   * Is process knowledge required?

   * Is knowledge of a particular readership's expectations required?

Activity Analysis

1. Student knowledge:

    *   How familiar are students with the specific form and conventions associated with a particular kind of writing and particular community of readers? What experiences will allow students to express a quality standard for the kind of writing they will attempt to produce?

    *   How prepared are students to generate the kind of text they will be attempting to compose? In other words, how ready are students to tell, define, analyze, argue, or follow any other thinking procedure associated with a writing effort? How can you structure experiences so that learners immerse themselves in the relevant processes and reflect on what they have done?

    *   Is it likely that all students know something about the subject of their writing? If not, what experiences will help the learners access the relevant information?

2. Resources:

    *   Can students readily access and sort the information they already have? If students already know a lot about a topic or problem, what means can they rely on to search, sort, and assess what they already know?

    *   What tools—classroom computers, Internet-enabled projection screens, photocopiers—does the school provide for accessing and distributing materials?

    *   What materials are available for the activities? What considerations affect their selection (cost, availability, labor involved, other constraints)?

3. Designing and sequencing activities:

    *   What sequences of activities will help students proceed from accessible materials and challenges to more complex tasks of the same type?

    *   How much instructional time is available for activities that teach students how to engage in task-related thinking and writing?

    *   What is the appropriate balance and sequence of individual, small-group, and whole-class instructional settings?

    *   In what ways does the instruction fit within the parameters and requirements of the broader curriculum?

An Example of a Structured Process Activity

We can illustrate this approach with an activity in which high school students, in groups, compare and contrast two similar but different restaurant menus before selecting one of the restaurants as the location for an anniversary party. The instructions identify two particular restaurants, but you can easily substitute the names of two local restaurants and use their menus. The menus should provide enough information to allow students to determine the extent to which each restaurant will meet the stated specifications.

◇◇◇◇◇◇◇◇◇◇◇◇◇◇   **THE ANNIVERSARY DINNER**   ◇◇◇◇◇◇◇◇◇◇◇◇◇◇◇◇◇◇

Introduction: Working in groups of three or four, you and your classmates will examine the similarities and differences in two pieces of information in order to advise an audience which one to choose. After studying and discussing the information, you will collaboratively compose a letter that offers your analysis and provides details to illustrate your general observations.

Audience: You will address your letter to Elizabeth and Mentor Latham, a couple who are planning a dinner party to celebrate their tenth wedding anniversary. They got married in their hometown (where your school is located), but they have been living in another state for the past eight years. They will return to their hometown to celebrate their tenth anniversary with their closest friends and their parents.

Purpose: Elizabeth and Mentor Latham remember how helpful you were in planning their wedding ten years ago. Now they have asked you, now in your thirties, to help them plan their tenth anniversary dinner. They recall the names of some of the best restaurants in town, but they realize that much may have changed during the past eight years. Elizabeth and Mentor asked you to visit and examine several of the best restaurants in town and narrow down the recommendations to just two choices. After investigating the finest of the local cuisine, you have narrowed your choices to Estelle's Kitchen and Cucina Katrina, and are now ready to examine their menus in detail in order to recommend one of these two restaurants to host the extravaganza (see Figure 2–2).

Specifications: Besides you and your guest, the Latham guest list for the dinner party includes:

The Wedding Party: Frank Envenes and guest
                           Bill Stugger (husband of Lela)
                           Lela Stugger (wife of Bill)

CHAPTER 2 A Structured Process Approach to Teaching Writing

>   Emil Karkaczyvski and guest
>   Anna Hiawatha and guest
>   Earla Pomgrief and guest

The Parents: Talbot Latham, father of groom
                    Esther Latham, mother of groom
                    Enrico Bottagaluppo, father of bride
                    Secunda Bottagaluppo, mother of bride

All told, including Elizabeth and Mentor and you and your guest, eighteen people will be attending the dinner.

Here are some additional details you need to consider:

- Frank Envenes is a strict vegetarian; he eats no meat or seafood and eats no food prepared or cooked with animal byproducts (cooked in animal fat, prepared with gelatin, etc.). He does, however, eat dairy products.

- Lela Stugger has asthma and cannot tolerate being in a room that has any trace of smoke.

- Emil Karkaczyvski cannot stand Italian food.

- Elizabeth Latham and her parents, Enrico and Secunda Bottagaluppo, love Italian food. Secunda, however, loves her own home-cooked Italian food and finds restaurant versions a poor substitute.

- Mr. Talbot Latham, Mentor's father, suffers from severe arthritis pain. He travels with the aid of a tubular frame walker and cannot climb stairs. He cannot walk long distances.

- Earla Pomgrief belongs to a religious sect whose strict dietary laws prevent her from eating fish or fowl. Also, she cannot eat organ meats or any kind of beef served with dairy products.

- Elizabeth and Mentor want to spend no more than thirty-five dollars per person, including beverage, tax, and gratuity.

Artifacts/materials: The two restaurants' menus are provided. In addition to describing the food items and their costs, the menus provide details about the atmosphere and accommodations at the restaurants.

Planning and drafting your written response: Before you compose your letter to Mr. and Mrs. Latham, you will want to do some talking and planning. Here are some suggestions for analyzing the problem with your partners:

- Decide on the important features you want to include in your analysis. The specifications will probably guide your decisions. For example, you might want to consider the price of the items in the various menu categories and the total cost per person. You might consider the types and variety of food and the accessibility of the facilities and how they match the guests' needs and preferences. You might also consider the restaurants' atmosphere and amenities in relation to this occasion.

- There are a variety of means you can use to plan your analysis: lists, a traditional outline, a word map, a tree diagram, a Venn diagram, mapping software, or some other organizational tool that allows you to see the similarities and differences.

- When organizing your letter, keep your audience and your purpose in mind. How much does the audience already know? Of what do you need to persuade them? What kinds of evidence will persuade them that your advice is sound enough to follow?

- Consider the transitional words and phrases you will use to make explicit connections between the two restaurants and their special features.

Reporting and revising: After you have planned your analysis and have written a rough draft, read your letter to other members of the class. Does anyone have questions or valid criticisms of your letter? Does your letter show your purpose for writing and reveal your appreciation for the needs of your audience? Have you provided enough specific details to allow others to see how you arrived at your conclusions about the similarities and differences? Have you provided smooth transitions so that it is easy for others to see references and connections?

Editing and completing a final draft: Your finished composition should take the form of a letter to your close friends Elizabeth and Mentor Latham, 711 Fortune's Way, Providence, Rhode Island. Elizabeth is an English teacher who is very critical of sloppy use of the English language. You will want to proofread carefully and make any necessary corrections before submitting your letter.

Variation: You may instead consider two real restaurants in your community. If you choose this option, you must have the menus from these restaurants available in class at our next meeting, and the restaurants should be appropriate settings for the anniversary dinner.

Reflection: After you have completed your letter, write a brief summary of this activity to help other writers who face a similar situation. Think about the process you followed to complete your letter successfully. How were you able to do this? As best you can, and in sufficient detail, explain how you thought about the problem, how you worked with your classmates, how you planned, how you generated a draft of the letter, and how you shaped it into a finished product.

ESTELLE'S KITCHEN
An American Restaurant
101 W. Martingdale Way

Estelle's Kitchen is a modern restaurant located in a quiet suburb. All dining areas are on the first floor. Banquet rooms, holding 20 to 250 people, are available. There is free valet parking, or diners can use the adjacent parking lot. All major credit cards are accepted. There is a 17% service/gratuity charge for all parties of ten or more. Estelle's Kitchen allows smoking only on the outdoor patio, which is accessible from the main dining area.

MENU

APPETIZERS

Estelle's Hot Wings—Deep-fried and tossed in Estelle's famous hot sauce **$7.95**
Smoked Salmon—Served with corn bread . . **$8.95**
Chicken Wings—Served with garlic and a blue cheese sauce **$5.50**
Basket of Sweet Potato Fries—Deep-fried in canola oil **$4.50**
Cheese Fries—Dripping with our four-cheese combo **$5.50**
Fries and Gravy—Made in our kitchen with savory brown gravy **$5.75**
Ask your server for our daily specials & soup of the day

ENTREES

Estelle's Kitchen entrees include a small dinner salad, soup of the day, and dinner rolls.
Fried Chicken—Estelle's famous fried chicken, with mashed potatoes and cole slaw . . . **$9.75**
Short Ribs—Smoked short ribs with baked beans or French fries **$9.95**
Fried Catfish—Fresh farm-raised catfish in light corn flour, battered and deep fried **$11.95**
Meat Loaf—Country meat loaf, baked with Estelle's own sweet and tangy sauce . . . **$9.95**
Stuffed Pork Chops—Made with our famous apple-walnut-cranberry stuffing . . . .
small portion $8.95 / large portion $11.95
Salisbury Steak—Served with mashed potatoes and vegetables **$10.95**
Baked Chicken—Slow-baked half-chicken, with roasted potatoes and vegetables **$10.95**
Roast Turkey—Roasted white and dark meat turkey, with sweet potatoes, stuffing, and vegetable **$10.95**
Liver with Bacon and Onions—Sautéed liver, with bacon, caramelized onions, and boiled potatoes **$9.95**

Pot Roast—Slow-cooked pot roast, with pan-roasted potatoes and vegetable **$10.95**

MEATLESS SPECIALTIES

Seafood Gumbo—A Southern tradition, highly seasoned, with a rich variety of seafood **$8.75**
Shrimp Creole—Smothered vegetables, with a spicy tomato sauce and shrimp, served with rice **$14.95**
Veggie Burger—Served on a whole-wheat bun, with fries and cole slaw **$8.75**
Macaroni and Cheese—Estelle's special recipe for baked macaroni and cheese, with a four-cheese mixture **$7.95**

BEVERAGES

Soft Drinks—unlimited refills of popular brands $2.00
Milk—plain, chocolate, or strawberry **$1.50**
Bottled Water—from Balbonian Mineral Springs $2.50
Fruit Juice—freshly prepared, your choice of blueberry, strawberry, kiwi, and peach . . **$3.50**
Vegetable Juice—celery, carrot, tomato, lima bean, or a blend **$4.00**
Coffee—regular or decaf **$2.50**
Tea—hot, sweet iced, or plain iced **$2.00**
Also see our wine list. Wine is served only to customers of proven legal drinking age.
Cost for house labels: **$7.00 per glass**

DESSERTS

Bread Pudding—Served in a warm vanilla sauce and topped with whipped cream **$5.75**
Apple Pie—Served with freshly whipped cream or ice cream, topped with cinnamon . . . **$5.75**
Key Lime Pie—Estelle's awarding winning pie **$5.95**

CUCINA KATRINA
1212 S. Tumbella Street

Cucina Katrina is operated by the O'Shaughnessy family in a restored two-story building in the warehouse district. Banquet rooms for parties of 15 to 100 are available on the second floor. Wheelchair access is provided to the second floor through a freight elevator in the kitchen. Valet parking is available for $7.00. Other parking is available in a lot one block south on Tumbella Street. The restaurant accepts most major credit cards. There is an automatic 15 percent gratuity added for parties of 10 or more. Smoking anywhere on the premises is strictly forbidden.

MENU

HOT APPETIZERS
Sautéed Zucchini—Slices of garden-fresh zucchini coated in egg batter and sautéed **$4.95**

Sautéed Shrimp—Whole shrimp sautéed in olive oil, garlic, and white wine **$10.95**

Twice Baked Clams—Clams, finely minced and twice baked with Italian herbs and spices **$7.95**

Baked Clams—Whole clams stuffed and baked . . **$7.95**

Broiled Shrimp—Stuffed shrimp broiled in their shell **$10.95**

Fried Calamari—Baby octopus fried till crispy golden brown and served with a tangy cocktail sauce **$7.95**

COLD APPETIZERS
Frutti Di Mare Alla Katrina—Marinated octopus, calamari, and cuttlefish **$7.95**

Bruschetta—Italian bread, brushed with olive oil, garlic, and herbs, topped with fresh tomatoes, basil, and cracked pepper **$5.95**

Salad Capri—Slices of fresh tomatoes, fresh mozzarella, olive oil, and fresh basil **$8.95**

Artichoke Salad—Marinated artichoke hearts . . . **$5.95**

Oysters on the Half Shell—Blue point oysters or clams, served in their shell **$9.50**

INSALATA
Seafood Salad—A mixture of shrimp, lobster, and crabmeat, served on Bibb lettuce **$16.95**

Spinach Salad—Leaf spinach with bacon, mushrooms, eggs, and a tangy oregano dressing **$7.95**

Tomato and Red Onion Salad—Slices of fresh tomatoes and thinly sliced red onions in balsamic vinaigrette **$8.95**

House Salad—Mixed greens, tomatoes, peppers, and olives **$8.95**

PASTA
Clam Spaghetti—Pasta served with clam sauce, red or white . . . . **side order $5.50 / full order $12.95**

Spaghetti, Penne, or Ravioli Alla Katrina—Pasta with Cucina Katrina's famous meat sauce **side order $5.00 / full order $12.95**

Spaghetti or Linguini with Garlic and Olive Oil—Pasta with olive oil, garlic, and parsley . . . **side order $5.00 / full order $12.95**

Cheese Ravioli or Green Fettuccini—Pasta with tomato sauce, anchovies, herbs, and spices **side order $5.00 / full order $12.95**

Linguini or Cheese Ravioli with Pesto Sauce—Pasta with a sauce of olive oil, basil, pine nuts, and grated cheese . . . . **side order $5.00 / full order $12.95**

Tortellini or Fettuccine Alfredo—Pasta with cream, eggs, and Parmesan cheese . . . . **side order $5.00 / full order $12.95**

Rigatoni alla Bolognese—Pasta with classic meat sauce . . . . **side order $5.00 / full order $12.95**

Lasagna—Layered pasta filled with meat sauce and ricotta cheese **$13.95**

SPECIALITA DELLA CASA
Baked Chicken—Half-chicken, slowly roasted with chopped garlic, celery, onions, herbs, and spices **$13.95**

Chicken Della Casa—Boneless breast of chicken in olive oil, garlic, and rosemary, with wild mushrooms **$15.95**

Chicken Parmesan—Boneless breast of chicken baked with our unique tomato sauce and zesty Parmesan cheese **$13.95**

Chicken Cacciatore—Sautéed chicken with tomatoes, mushrooms, and spices in a white wine sauce, served on a bed of spaghetti **$14.95**

Chicken alla Katrina—Sautéed boneless breast of chicken with peppers, mushrooms, and tomatoes **$14.95**

Chicken with Zucchini—Pan-fried boneless breast of chicken with zucchini and mushrooms **$14.95**

Eggplant Parmesan—Baked eggplant, mozzarella cheese, and tomato sauce . . . **$12.95**

Pan Fried Steak—Butterflied sirloin steak, tomatoes, onions, and green peppers . . . **$22.95**

Veal Wrapped in Ham—Thin slices of veal sautéed and garnished with Parma ham **$19.95**

Veal Parmesan—Veal baked with mozzarella cheese and tomatoes **$18.95**

Veal Katrina—Thin slices of veal sautéed in butter, garlic, spices, peppers, mushrooms, and pimento **$19.95**

SEAFOOD

Broiled Lake Superior Whitefish Almandine—Baked in butter, with sliced almonds **$17.95**

Broiled Red Snapper—Served with butter and sliced almond sauce **$19.95**

French Fried Gulf Shrimp—Deep fried shrimps **$19.95**

Garlic Shrimp—Jumbo shrimps broiled with garlic sauce **$19.95**

Sautéed Shrimp—Prepared with olive oil, butter, and garlic **$19.95**

Calamari Marinara—Squid sautéed with tomatoes, garlic, herbs, and spices **$14.95**

Seafood Stew—Shrimps, mussels, clams, and squid sautéed in tomatoes, garlic, extra virgin olive oil, and white wine **$19.95**

BEVERAGES

Soft Drinks—cola, lemon-lime, or orange soda; diet or regular . . . **$1.50 per serving; no refills**

Goat Milk—fresh, tart, and delicious; whole or skim **$3.50**

Sparkling Bottled Water—from the Buenos Agua Aquifer **$3.50**

Coffee—regular or decaf **$2.50**

Latté—regular or decaf **$4.00**

Espresso—regular or decaf **$4.00**

Cappuccino—regular or decaf **$4.00**

Tea—hot, herbal, caffeinated, sweet iced, or plain iced **$2.00**

We also have a wine list. You must be of legal drinking age to order from this menu.

Cost for house labels: **$7.50 per glass**

DESSERTS

Assorted Italian Ices—Available in kiwi, watermelon, raspberry, lemon, and orange creme **$3.50**

Cheese Cake—Your choice of pecan caramel, goat cheese with mixed berries, strawberry, apple cinnamon, pumpkin, chocolate, and mint **$6.50**

Spumoni—A Naples tradition, made with pistachios, chocolate, and cherry bits **$4.00**

Cannoli—A Sicilian favorite, available in vanilla, chocolate, or pistachio **$4.00**

Napoleon—A layered crispy puff pastry, available in traditional, chocolate, almond, or berry **$6.00**

Tiramisu—Thick lady fingers dipped in coffee and served with mascarpone cream **$6.50**

All Entrees include choice of Chicken Broth or Minestrone
House Salad and Dessert
Garlic Bread Served upon Request

What Makes This Sequence a Structured Process Approach?

The activity has these features of structured process instruction:

1. A "real world" problem identifies a compelling purpose and a specific audience.

2. There is a body of information to analyze in order to solve the problem.

3. Structured discussion stages encourage learners to plan and revise collaboratively.

4. The problem allows for various visualization and organizational strategies.

5. Quality criteria are explicit but open to negotiation and interpretation.

6. A reflection component fosters metacognition and the future ability to apply the process in similar instances.

This activity involves students in one kind of writing in one context. However, when embedded in a curriculum offering a variety of writing and learning experiences, it will expand their repertoire of problem-solving strategies and composing procedures in relation to any comparison and contrast task.

Student groups can approach the problem in a variety of ways. In general, however, they will refer to their overall purpose and use the inherent constraints to guide their analysis of the relevant information. Some students calculate the average cost per person; others make subjective judgments about the quality of the food. When students write about the situation, they usually have a lot to say. They know their "stuff"—the content germane to this problem. They are also using specific strategies for a particular context. They do not compare and contrast for the sake of comparing and contrasting; they use various analyses as a tool for accomplishing a goal. In the end, it is not important which recommendation the students make, as long as they justify their choice. It is important, however, that they think in conjunction with others and develop procedures they can use independently in other situations and with other information.

By deliberately working through several stages in order to produce an immediate product, the students have an opportunity to make a good decision. If they make their procedures explicit, they will be able to apply them to other situations that require comparisons and contrasts, situations in which they work independently and gather their own information. Students have access to the "stuff" of composition. They address a particular problem, work with specific problem-solving strategies, and have opportunities to rehearse their compositions in their discussions with other students before they put their ideas on paper.

Preparing students to write well-developed, thoughtful compositions is time consuming. This activity does not address all the considerations in completing a task as complicated and interactive as writing. Realistically, before the students are able to apply specific skills and strategies to new situations, they will need several experiences and appropriate feedback, both from other students and from their teacher or other readers. Chapter 6 provides a much more detailed sequence of activities for teaching comparison and contrast writing.

On to Part 2

The chapters that follow show you how to apply a structured process approach to writing instruction in a number of genres. They include examples of activities that elicit the substantive conversations and thinking processes that are essential for learning how to write in a variety of situations. In most instances, we have reproduced the discussions that resulted, and we present samples of the writing that students produced. We hope you will be able to use these same principles to develop structured process instruction that suits the needs of your school, classroom, and students. Some of the teachers we present are either real individuals or based on teachers we know; others are composites of several teachers who have used these activities in their classrooms. The instruction that we present, whether based on one or many individuals, follows from classroom realities and students' discussion, activity, and writing in response to the teaching.

Questions for Reflection

Think of a time you were assigned a writing task with which you had difficulty.

1. What was the task?

2. What kind of preparation were you given for writing it (e.g., an assignment, a model to follow, time for planning, strategies for planning, freewriting, suggestions for topics, explicit instruction in how to write it, etc.)?

3. What time frame were you given to complete the task?

4. Were you given opportunities to work on your writing during school?

5. Were you given opportunities to discuss your writing with anyone else at different points in your writing process? If so, when, under what circumstances, and to what effect?

6. When, if ever, did you have an opportunity to work in partnership with a classmate or classmates to produce a piece of writing? What was the task, and how did you manage the partnership?

7. Did you have opportunities to revise your writing based on feedback from others?

8. Do you feel that you would be able to produce writing of a similar type in the future, based on your experience with this writing? Why or why not?

9. What did you learn from the writing experience?

10. In retrospect, how would your level of difficulty with the task have been reduced through different instruction?

11. If you were to assign students writing of this type, how would you go about it so that the greatest number of students has a chance to succeed?

12. How did technology play a role in your learning to write and in your effort to compose?

Theory in Practice
Teaching Writing
Using a Structured Sequence
of Activities

CHAPTER

3

Teaching
Fictional Narratives

Narrative fiction constitutes the bulk of what is *read* in most English and language arts curriculums, yet *writing* narrative fiction remains among the least often experienced genres in our classrooms. Applebee and Langer (2006) report on the relative degree to which analysis/ interpretation, summaries, reports, journals, persuasive writing, and stories are taught. Among the genres taught to eighth graders, story writing ties for last place with logs/journals and persuasion; for high school seniors, story writing is dead last. In school students are strongly encouraged to read stories but not to write them. This discrepancy seems odd to say the least.

Yet in their lives outside school, students produce all manner of creative writing, from fan fiction on the Internet (Black 2008) to stories and poems by students who are barely passing in school (Schultz 2002). Writing fictional narratives is therefore a ripe area for classroom instruction. Let's observe as Ms. Alva (composite) attempts it in her classroom. Ms. Alva follows the example represented by Betsy Jo Hansen in the sixth scenario in Chapter 1, and expands on the lesson to reveal the detailed thinking involved in the teacher's plans and decisions.

Task Analysis

A key assumption behind a structured process approach is that each writing situation poses its own demands and expectations. To spell out the possible challenges, a teacher might ask, *"What do my students need to know and what do they need to be able to do in order to write a successful fictional narrative?"*

A task analysis also considers the task in connection with the characteristics of the learners and the broader setting of their writing. This setting includes who will be reading it, what those readers expect, which conventions are appropriate for the task and situation, what is appropriate for carrying out this writing in school, and other factors. The question about the writer's knowledge assumes that the teacher knows quite a bit about the students: what they know about writing generally, what they know about the form and conventions of writing fictional narratives, and what they know about the procedures for producing both this and other types of composition.

Ms. Alva's explicit goal for this series of lessons is for students "to produce fictional suspense stories that provide descriptive details to create the appropriate mood, elicit an empathic response from the reader, and follow a logical development." She can assume that her students have an abundance of knowledge, both about suspense stories as a kind of narrative and about subjects and situations appropriate for their own stories. This knowledge of content and form, however, does not guarantee that students will be able to write their own stories. What they need—and what a structured process approach is designed to teach them—is a set of *procedures for how to write* such stories.

Ms. Alva decides she needs a provocative prompt that will spark her students' imaginations by establishing a setting and an impetus and suggesting a number of ways to bring their narratives to life. She finds a pdf file of a photograph of a deserted alley that she believes her students will find stimulating (see Figure 3–1). Although the photo by itself will probably work, she believes it will be more effective if accompanied by sounds that will trigger spine-tingling images. On the Internet she finds sounds that are ideal for this purpose (www.thefreesite.com/Free_Sounds/Free_WAVs/), including cars stopping and going on wet pavement, footsteps advancing and retreating, and a metallic rattling like a dumpster lid opening and closing. She saves them on her digital recorder to play as she projects the alley image on a screen. Ms. Alva is ready to proceed.

Figure 3–1.
Scene of a
deserted alley

Stage 1. Generating Task-Specific Evaluative Criteria

Structured process pedagogy involves drawing students' attention to the qualities that characterize writing of the type they are undertaking. Because different types of tasks call for different qualities—an argument and a fable draw on different conventions and uses of language—each task requires specific attention to evaluative criteria.

In writing instruction, teachers typically provide models of successful compositions for students to imitate (Hillocks 1986). Such models are usually offered with little attention to the procedures that students should employ to produce similar pieces of writing. A structured process approach is more oriented to procedures. Samples of student writing may come into play in the generation of criteria but rather than using them as "models" to imitate, a teacher uses them as texts for students to evaluate. Students produce criteria by examining a mixed set of fictional narratives and determining which qualities they wish to emulate in their own writing. The samples are not final destinations at which students should arrive but rather texts to consider as they generate their own criteria.

Before the students begin writing, Ms. Alva wants them to understand the expectations readers often have for fictional narratives with suspenseful elements. She tells her students that over a series of days they will be writing a story that has many of the features of the stories they will be reading and discussing in class. When the stories are finished, volunteers will read theirs to the class and all the stories will be collected in a volume that will remain in the classroom until the end of the year and then be donated to the school library. (There is also the option of posting the collection to Ms. Alva's school website if the students agree.)

Ms. Alva then reads three stories (see Story 1, Story 2, and Story 3 that follow) to the class. Afterward, in groups of three or four, the students spend about ten minutes listing the features that the three stories have in common and ranking the stories from best to worst. These discussions produce a list of suspense-story features and identify qualities readers of suspense stories expect and enjoy.

Story 1

My aunt came to visit us and stay at our house for the weekend. When my aunt came into the house, she left her heavy suitcase at the top of the landing that leads to the basement. Later that night, when my mom and my aunt were drinking tea and talking at the kitchen table, they thought they heard someone pounding on our back door. My mom and aunt freaked out, because no one usually knocks on the back door.

They were afraid to open the back door, so they got a flashlight and shined it out of the window and into the backyard. Finally, my mom got our little dog (9 lbs.) and set the phone to speed dial 911. My mom went out the front door and searched around the house to see if she could find who was pounding on the door. She couldn't see anyone.

When Mom came in again, my aunt asked where her suitcase was. We saw that it was at the bottom of the stairs to the basement. It fell down the stairs and must have made a pounding noise that made us think that someone was banging on the back door.

Story 2

We heard the sound of "crunch, crunch, crunch" coming from behind us in the dark woods that surrounded our campsite. Suddenly my heart pounded in my chest like a hammer banging against a wall. "What's that?" I asked my dad and my friend Chris.

Chris said nothing, but my dad tried to be calm: "It was probably a dead tree limb that fell in the woods, or it may be some little animal like a squirrel."

I stood up and looked around. "No, Dad. It sounded like something a lot heavier than a squirrel. What do you think it could be?" I tried to look into the dark woods, but the light from our campfire couldn't penetrate the dark around the trees. I stood in a small circle of light, with the darkness surrounding us.

"If it will make you feel better," my dad said, "I'll take a look."

He got up from his seat on a log near the fire and grabbed a flashlight. The thought of my dad going into the woods alone and leaving Chris and me behind paralyzed me. "Wait, Dad. Let's listen to hear it again."

By now, Chris was standing, too. The three of us stood close by the fire, casting long narrow shadows that reached into the darkness of the woods. The fire hissed and popped, and the breeze moved smoke from the fire to wrap around us. Breezes stirred dead leaves that seemed to chase after each other and dance in circles. As we tried to be as still as possible, my heart raced and rushed blood to my ears, making a muffled booming noise. I heard something else, which could have been Chris whimpering.

"This is silly," said Dad. "I'm going to see if there is anything there."

Once my dad has made up his mind, there is no stopping him. He moved quickly into the woods, with the hazy beam of light from his flashlight leading the way.

Chris finally spoke. "Maybe we should wait in the truck," he said.

I agreed, but I didn't want to seem too panicked. "Let's just wait here by the fire," I said.

We stood there for a long time, and the fire was beginning to die down. I put a couple of small logs on the fire, to keep up the light and to give me something to do. My dad was gone for a long time. Then I heard the "crunch, crunch, crunch" again. "Chris, did you hear that?" I asked.

"I hear something walking toward us," said Chris. You could see him tense up, like a hedgehog rolling itself into a ball. I think that if we were a little bit younger, he would have grabbed my arm for support.

"Is that you, Dad?" I called out. No answer. "Dad, we're over here," I shouted.

"Yeah, we're over here," Chris yelled. No answer.

We looked into the woods all around us. It was like trying to read something at the bottom of a cup of coffee. In the distance we saw a dim light dancing around. "Look. What's that?" I asked Chris.

"I don't know, but I wish your dad was back."

I went to the truck and got another flashlight from the glove compartment. I started to flash it in the direction of the other light, moving the light back and forth. The light in the woods also moved back and forth as if to imitate my movement. As I watched, the light in the woods seemed to get closer and closer. I wanted that light to be my dad returning to the campsite, but I wasn't sure. I grabbed Chris by the shoulder and we moved to the far side of the campsite and waited.

We watched the light move closer and closer, until Dad finally came out of the woods and into the glow of the campfire. "Thank goodness you flashed that flashlight into the woods. I lost my way back to the campsite and I thought I'd have to make a bed on the leaves in the woods. You helped me find my way back. But I couldn't find anything out there, so let's put out the fire and go to bed."

We were so happy to see my dad return and so relieved that we were glad to crawl into our sleeping bags. With the campfire out, there was no more hiss and pop, and the breeze died down. Dad and Chris quickly went to sleep in the tent. I was just about to fall asleep myself, when I heard, "crunch, crunch, crunch."

Story 3

There was an old woman who lived in my neighborhood. My friends and I didn't know her name. She looked really old. She wore ragged old clothes. No matter what the weather, her outdoor clothes always included a scarf and a heavy cloth overcoat with a wide and ragged collar. The rumor in the neighborhood was that she was a witch.

She lived in a wooden frame house, one story with an attic. All the windows were covered, with newspapers or curtains or even boards. It would be impossible to look in, even if one had the courage to do it. The house hadn't been painted in years, and it looked gray and brown and weather-beaten, almost like the old woman herself. Everyone knew that the house was filled with hundreds of stray dogs and cats. No one saw the woman walk a dog or sit on her porch with a cat in her lap, but you could see her buying a lot of pet food at the supermarket. And even outside the house it smelled like animal waste.

One afternoon, as I passed her house with a couple of my friends, my buddy Dennis said, "Watch this." He then walked up the three steps to the old woman's wooden porch and jumped up and down. The banging on the wooden porch set off an uproar of dog howls, cat screams, scrambling paws, overturned furniture, and scraping claws. There was no way to tell the number of animals inside the house, but it sounded as if there were hundreds. The house fairly rocked with the barks and cries. It was like having a live, wild doorbell.

We moved a few yards away from the house and waited for the noise to stop. Dennis then went back to the porch and pounded on it again. There was another uproar. The windows rattled, and the door shook under the weight of dozens of dogs hurtling themselves against it.

Soon the noise stopped again; then Dennis approached me and said, "Why don't you try it?" I wasn't sure. The first time might have caught the old woman by surprise. The second time might also have caught her by surprise, with the woman thinking, "No one would pull the same prank twice." At the third attempt she might be waiting, maybe preparing to unleash several attack dogs.

I slowly began walking up the creaking wooden stairs. As I reached the second step, Dennis half-whispered, "I'll watch the windows and the back." I hadn't thought about needing a lookout. As I crouched to begin my jump, Dennis yelled, "She's coming out the back. She's got two dogs."

I leaped over the rail of the porch and began running in the direction where Dennis had already fled. I knew that if the old lady were leading dogs on a leash, they would never come close to catching us. But I worried about her unleashing the dogs, and I believed that I heard the panting of dogs and the scraping of claws on the concrete walk behind me. I ran all the way home and into my yard. I closed the fence gate behind me and gasped for breath. But I didn't see or hear any dogs.

Two days later, I was at the grocery store with my mom. While my mom was at the deli counter, the old woman came up to me as I leaned against the shopping cart and whispered, "I'll get you next time."

- -

After the students have discussed their observations and judgments, Ms. Alva calls on representatives from each group to report their conclusions about the common features and their judgments about what distinguishes a good story. As the students contribute, Ms. Alva lists all the features on the overhead projector, rephrasing some and filtering others. For example, a student accurately notes that all three stories involve animals. Ms. Alva asks, "Is that fact *coincidental* or *essential* to all of the stories? In other words, do you think that all stories of this kind have to have animals in them?" Limiting themselves to essential elements, the students arrive at this list of characteristics:

EPISODE 1.2

There is something weird or unknown.
Something or someone poses a threat to the main character.
The main character feels frightened or threatened.
The reader worries that something bad might happen to the main character.

There is enough descriptive detail for the reader to imagine the characters, setting, and action.

The events of the story follow a logical order.

The story often includes dialogue.

Ms. Alva adds the last item herself and asks her learners what *dialogue* is and why it might contribute to the story.

Ms. Alva then tells the students the stories they are going to write must have all the features that appear on the list. In other words, the list comprises the directions for the assignment, as well as the evaluation criteria for grading it. Based on her previous teaching experience, Ms. Alva adds two constraints:

1. The story must be realistic enough to give the reader the feeling that the events could happen to anyone. In other words, the writers must avoid wild exaggerations, supernatural interventions, and outrageous parodies.

2. Violence must be downplayed. The suspense should derive from the sense of dread or foreboding, not from firing machine guns, exploding bombs, or slashing knives.

Stage 2. Gateway Activity: Establishing the Setting and Conflict

A hallmark of a structured process approach to writing instruction is to include a *gateway* (Hillocks 1995) or *introductory* (Smagorinsky et al. 1987) activity. A gateway activity gives students a clear framework for the task ahead. Often the gateway activity helps students develop a *cognitive map*, or schematic understanding of the task. Other gateway activities, such as the one that follows, stimulate student writing by furnishing a setting and suggesting specific details.

EPISODE 2.1 Ms. Alva darkens the classroom and projects a picture of a deserted alley (see Figure 3–1). In the photo, a series of dumpsters lines up against the buildings from the left to the center of the photo. The windows of one building are boarded up. To the right, a padlock holds a set of metal doors secure. It appears as though the alley leads to another, although it's difficult to tell if there is a way out, or if this is a dead end.

Ms. Alva asks the students to list all the words they can think of that might appear in a story set in this alley. She encourages the students to include action words. After a couple of minutes, Ms. Alva calls on volunteers to share their words; she lists them on a transparency as they do so. This list, which follows, gets students thinking about the substance of a suspense story, helps them generate a plot line, and becomes a convenient word bank from which to draw when writing descriptions.

WORD LIST

drip	alarm
footsteps	bouncing
creaky	door closing
clump	creaking
splash	echoes
puddle	horrible
alley cat	pop out
screech	rattle
racing cars	flies
v-roooom	buzzing
slamming doors	skunk
scream	rotten eggs
high-pitched	body
siren	damp
mist	fog

After generating this preliminary set of words/images, Ms. Alva introduces a second prewriting activity to help students imagine themselves in the setting they've begun to develop. She asks them to imagine that they or a fictional character of their choice is alone and crouched between two of the dumpsters. She then plays a sound recording of street noises (e.g., cars coming and going, a dog pattering by, etc.) and of footsteps on wet pavement growing louder and more distinct as they approach. Working individually at first, the students jot down ideas about other sounds they might hear in the alley, the smells around them, and the emotions they would experience.

EPISODE 2.2

At this point, Ms. Alva prompts her students to write a description of the setting: "You will want to help your reader see, hear, smell, and feel whatever the character would be experiencing in the situation. In your description, bring the setting to life. It will be helpful to rely on vivid verbs and striking comparisons. Keep in mind some of the words and phrases from our word bank."

Ms. Alva gives her students about fifteen minutes to compose the descriptions. Then she asks volunteers to share what they've written. She listens especially for the verbs and the comparisons. She encourages all the students to continue to develop their description, paying special attention to verbs and comparisons.

EPISODE 2.3 With the setting of the students' fictional narratives established, Ms. Alva needs to help her students identify an essential conflict. She directs the students, in groups of three, to discuss possible conflicts that could develop when a stranger approaches someone. She gives three examples: a dreaded enemy is seeking revenge, a law enforcement officer is searching for an escapee, or a mobster is seeking to bump off a rival. As the students suggest other possibilities, their partners approve or disapprove. Some suggest variations and details or question the feasibility of the situation. Others wonder if the situation might be less sinister—someone looking for a lost dog or coming to throw some trash in the dumpster. Through this process, they began to generate and refine their plot lines.

Stage 3. Language Lesson: Attention to Dialogue

In a structured process approach, grammar, mechanics, and usage are addressed in the context of student writing rather than in disembodied exercises. Ms. Alva therefore has developed an exercise to teach students the conventions for using and punctuating dialogue (see Figure 3–2): how to convert indirect quotations into direct quotations, where to place end punctuation in relation to quotation marks, and how to begin a new paragraph to indicate a shift in speaker. She distributes the handout and guides the students through the items. (If students are learning these writing conventions for the first time, she may have the students do the activities in pairs or small groups rather than individually.)

Stage 4. From Group to Individual: Drafting the Narratives

Before Ms. Alva has her students begin their drafts, she returns their attention to the first paragraph in each of the three stories they have examined. She asks about the differences among the story openings. Students volunteer that one story begins with a sound and action, another with a simple description of the setting. Ms. Alva asks which opening appeals to them most as readers. She reminds them that they have several options for how to begin the story.

Next, each student begins drafting a story, paying special attention to details that will bring the situation and setting to life for the reader. Some students continue to work on the story at home.

Figure 3–2. Presenting Dialogue

There are accepted ways in which to present *dialogue*, a word that refers to what people say in a story. The following exercises present a few simple rules for presenting characters' dialogue in your stories.

1. Converting an *indirect quotation* to a *direct quotation*

The following sentence provides a summary of what someone has said:

Daryl B. Trouble told me to go home.

This is known as an *indirect quotation* because Daryl's exact words are not reproduced; rather, they are summarized. In contrast, a *direct quotation* goes within *quotation marks* and reports exactly what someone has said, as in the following sentence:

Daryl B. Trouble told me, "Go home, fool!"

Rewrite each of the following five sentences so that the indirect quotation is presented as a direct quotation.

1. Roland Butter asked me when the soup would be ready.

2. At the beginning of class, the teacher told us to turn in our homework.

3. I got an email saying that I had just won a million dollars.

4. Bette DeRanch said that we should keep the noise down.

5. The principal congratulated us for being so well behaved.

2. Punctuating quotations

In the United States, punctuation usually goes *inside* the closing quotation mark of a direct quotation, as in the following sentences:

"I am a happy camper."

"Those are delicious lima beans," said Jim Panzee.

Lauren Order shouted, "I'm free at last!"

"How did you do that?" asked the magician's assistant.   *(continues)*

Figure 3–2. Presenting Dialogue *(continued)*

In the following sentences, place both quotation marks and punctuation in the proper locations:

1. We might be behind by 50 points, but we will win the game said the coach.

2. The chef exclaimed This is my greatest creation ever!

3. Why do you want me to do that I asked my mother.

4. The mayor declared No dog shall roam this town unleashed.

5. Ginger Snapps was told No more cookies for you by the cafeteria lady.

3. **Quotations and paragraphs**

A final rule regarding quotations in stories is that every time a new speaker begins, the writer should start a new paragraph. When two or more characters are speaking, the proper form looks like this:

"Hello!" said Ira Fuse to Kareem O'Wheat.

"And a big howdy to you!" replied Kareem.

Ira paused and asked, "What are you up to?"

Kareem paused to think. He then said, "I was just about to head into that dark and shadowy alley to see if anything pops out and tries to scare me."

"Great idea," said Ira. "What do you say we hide between those two dumpsters and see what happens?"

Kareem smiled and replied, "That's a fantastic idea! Last one in is a rotten egg."

"What a coincidence," said Ira. "It rather smells of rotten eggs in a rancid, fetid, repulsive sort of way."

"Well then," said Kareem, "I think we're doing the right thing."

"What could possibly go wrong?" inquired Ira as they headed in to crouch between the dumpsters and enjoy the remainder of the afternoon.

Stage 5. From Individual to Group: Peer Response to First Drafts

When the students' first drafts are complete, Ms. Alva devotes some class time to helping students learn how to critique one another's writing for the purpose of revising their initial efforts. She models the process using a former student's essay (with the name removed), which she projects on the overhead. Together the students and Ms. Alva check that the story has all the features they have decided are essential to a suspense story. She focuses on elements covered in her instruction, because she knows that trying to consider every aspect of good writing will overwhelm her young writers. Hypercorrection might undermine their ability to learn the specific strategies for producing suspenseful, fictional narratives that she has been teaching.

EPISODE 5.1

The students now exchange the drafts of their stories with a partner and together review their attempts and recommend revisions based on what they believe would make the story more suspenseful and riveting for the reader. Their peer critiques follow this structure (provided by Ms. Alva):

EPISODE 5.2

1. The writer slowly reads the story aloud to his or her partner.

2. Each partner tells the other, "The thing I liked most about your story was . . . ."

3. Each partner points out any essential story elements that are missing and what might be included to make the story more engaging. The focus is on helping writers compose effectively within the narrative genre rather than on simply filling in categories.

4. Each student reads his or her partner's story silently. With the writer's permission, the reader corrects errors in spelling, punctuation, and indention, paying special attention to the conventions for punctuating dialogue.

Stage 6. Completing and Publishing the Narratives

The revision process continues through two drafts, and the students "publish" their stories in a class collection. Some student volunteers read their stories aloud to the class; others invite Ms. Alva to read their story aloud for them. "Lost Dog" and "Never Coming Back" are typical of the suspense stories that most students in the class have produced.

EPISODE 6.1

"Lost Dog" by Sarah Knighton

I was rushing to get ready! It was cold out and my mom told me I had to wear layers of clothes. I hate wearing layers of clothes but I had to obey my mom, unfortunately! It looked like it was about to rain. Every Halloween I had to go trick-or-treating with my mom, but at least this year I get to go with my friends, too. I go to my grandma's almost every Halloween before I go trick-or-treating. It stinks because my grandma lives all the way in Chicago. I told my mom that I was ready and we started on our way to Chicago. I was looking out the window when I noticed it was getting really dark out and it started to rain. My grandma lives in an apartment by an alley. We finally got there and I ran into the apartment because I didn't want to get my costume wet. My mom had parked the car and came inside by me. Then I rang the doorbell. I saw the light turn on and I could hear my grandma's footsteps.

My grandma said, "Who is it?"

I said, "Grandma, it's me."

She opened the door and said, "Oh, it's my little clown!" I smiled. She said that because I was a clown for Halloween. We got inside and sat down in the living room. My stomach was making a funny noise. I asked my grandma if I could have something to eat. She nodded her head and continued to talk to my mom. So I went to the kitchen and grabbed the last packet of fruit snacks. I went over to throw out the box when I noticed that the garbage can was full. I told my grandma and she asked me if I could take the garbage out. I hesitated and said, "Well, okay."

I didn't want to go because the dumpster was in the alley and it was dark out. I walked outside, I was nervous and I was getting the goose bumps. I got into the alley and felt a rain drop dripping down my forehead. My knees were shaking. I threw out the bag. I heard something and looked over my left shoulder. I saw a dog. The dog was dripping wet and smelled very bad. She was very small and was limping so I think her leg was broken. I think she was afraid of me because she was slowly backing away. I heard footsteps coming toward me. I quickly grabbed the dog and hid in between the two dumpsters.

I heard a voice. "Roxie!" the voice called.

"Yikes!" I whispered.

I could hear the footsteps slowly going away. I peeked out into the alley. I couldn't see anyone. I slowly walked to the apartment door. I walked inside thinking of what to say to my mom. I looked down at the dog, and she was shivering.

I shouted to my mom from the kitchen, "Mom, can I see you in the kitchen?"

She said, "I will be there in a minute."

My heart was beating so fast, I felt like it was going to jump out of my body. My mom finally came in and I quickly said something before she could yell at me.

I said, "You see, Mom, I was taking out the garbage and I saw this dog. It looked like it was hurt so I picked it up. Please, oh, please, can I keep it!"

My mom looked puzzled. Then she said, "Did you hear anything or see anything in the alley?"

I didn't want to tell my mom. I knew I had to, though.

Slowly I said, "Well, I did hear footsteps and someone call the name Roxie." I looked down, thinking that I was holding Roxie. There was a long silence; then my mom said, "Why don't we go back to the alley and see if the person is still there." I agreed.

We walked down to the alley together. I got the goose bumps again.

My mom said, "Well, I guess we have to keep her." I smiled. I looked down at Roxie but she wasn't there.

"Never Coming Back" by Perri Brinkmeier

Amy and Peter were walking back from the local coffee shop at 9:00 at night. It was cold, rainy, and mysterious. They were planning on taking the long way home just when Amy said, "Let's take the short cut through the alley."

"That creepy thing?" Peter asked. "Are you sure it won't be long?"

"It won't be more than two minutes," Amy explained.

"Are you sure?" Peter asked nervously.

"You're just a chicken!" Amy taunted.

"I am not!" Peter shouted and went unhappily along with Amy.

Peter took his first steps into the alley. The wind started to howl and Peter stuttered, "I'm going back!"

Amy stopped him. "Oh, come on. You'll be fine."

They were in the middle of the alley when they heard glass breaking. They looked up and in one of the windows of the apartment building they saw a man in black clothes and a black mask holding a bag.

"Aaaaahhhhhhhhhhhh," they screamed. The man in black heard them and ran down the back stairs chasing them. He dropped the black bag, but didn't notice it. Amy and Peter kept running until they went around the corner and found a place to hide. The man ran past them and Peter whispered intensely, "I'M GOING HOME!"

"Why? Isn't this fun? We can look at what he hid in the bag!" Amy questioned.

"No, you were wrong once and you're going to be wrong again!" Peter whispered angrily.

"Fine. I'll stay here alone! You go home!"

"I will," Peter said and started running home. Amy walked back to get the bag, but the man was coming back!

"What will I do?" Amy said to herself. She hid between two dumpsters and watched what the mystery man did.

"Where's the bag?" the guy whispered to himself. Amy heard a voice, but the man's lips weren't moving. There must be another man. Amy thought she heard his name was Rob.

Rob whispered, "Who's the jewelry from?"

"Mrs. Gory," said the other man in his dark voice. "She's like 85 years old and she lives by herself. Let's go back to Mrs. Gory's house tomorrow night."

They finally left. Amy thought they never would. It really stinks between those dumpsters.

Later that night Amy called Mrs. Gory to warn her about the two men who were going to come the next night. Amy asked Mrs. Gory if she would like her to be there.

Mrs. Gory called the police station. "I want to report a robbery. My jewels were stolen last night. And they are coming back tonight to steal more!"

The police were interested. "We will DEFINITELY be there! Wait for us."

Mrs. Gory was writing all this down so she could remember.

That night, Amy and Mrs. Gory were waiting for the police to come. Minutes passed, hours passed, and they were still waiting. Mrs. Gory went up to the door and listened. She heard voices and recognized them from the police department, so she opened the door to let them in.

But instead of the police, Mrs. Gory and Amy saw two men wearing black. And that was the end of Mrs. Gory and Amy.

EPISODE 6.2   Soon after the class completes their stories, Ms. Alva tells her students how impressed she is with the quality of their work. She asks them to write a brief letter to her explaining what helped them write such good stories. Ms. Alva believes that by prompting this expansion of the students' thinking about their stories, she is promoting an awareness of the processes that the learners can rely on to produce similar narratives in the future. Here are three reflections:

I relished the sounds that you had on the tape and the sounds you helped us come up with. But most of all, I enjoyed the making of the story. As you know, it is always hard to get started. But once you've started, you get the idea and you can keep going. . . . One thing that I didn't think was necessary was the picture of the alley. It was helpful a little bit. Although I bet we still could have imagined it.

—Kerri

I liked when you played the sound! That really gave me my idea of a man walking through an alley taking very slow steps. The picture gave me an idea of what the setting of my story would be like! Those three stories you read us helped a lot! Now I know that a scary story is not about violence but is about getting the reader's heart pounding.

—Maggie

The three stories helped me know what the story should be like. Sharing our ideas in a small group was fun. It helped me develop a base idea for the story.

—Eric

Extensions

1. Collect the students' writing into an anthology that is available in the classroom and ultimately the school library. This activity might include teaching students how to bind the collection for durability and posterity. To help the students learn more about technology, have them convert the anthology to html or pdf files linked to your school website or perhaps from the school library's website.

2. Link the writing to the curriculum's oral speech strand by having students produce one-act plays based on narratives. Students could also film their performances. They could embellish these performances by constructing sets, choosing costumes, creating a soundtrack, and exploring other aspects of stage and film production. Link filmed productions to your school website. This public sharing encourages students to post comments and other artifacts in response to the stories, as they would on social networking websites.

3. Link the students' narratives to other reading they do in class.

What Makes This Sequence a Structured Process Approach?

Ms. Alva's lessons reveal much about the thinking that drives her planning. She begins by analyzing what she is asking her students to do, considering who her learners are, and assessing the degree to which their existing knowledge about content and procedures will help them meet the demands of the task.

In planning specific activities and organizing their sequence, Ms. Alva pays attention to features that make up a narrative: having a story to tell; drawing on personal experiences to support the development of the story; recognizing the specific form, conventions, and quality standards of a fictional suspense narrative; and generating detailed descriptions and narration. Ms. Alva's structured stages, often involving collaboration or peer response, are to prompt interest; generate ideas; plan a composition; write an initial draft; review, assess, and refine efforts; and share with peers.

While Ms. Alva reflects on the learners and their task as she begins planning, she also reacts and adjusts along the way, so that the instructional design is organic, following new paths and pacing as the lessons progress. Ms. Alva knows she must adjust the plan to the task and to the specific instructional circumstances; one lesson template does not fit every situation.

Ms. Alva also shares and co-plans with her colleagues, who ask questions and offer suggestions and variations. The entire team benefits, especially if teachers observe each other as they teach the lessons.

Questions for Reflection

1. What place does the writing of fiction narrative have in the middle school and high school writing curriculum?

2. The telling of stories relies often on invention. To what extent is it possible to teach students how to invent the substance of their narratives?

3. Describe the processes that a writer would follow in producing a work of fiction. To what extent would the composing process for a work of fiction be different from the composing process for a persuasive letter or an explanatory report?

4. The writing of memorable works of fiction relies on the writer's ability to make characters, settings, and action come alive for readers. How can a teacher help students refine their skills at description as an element in narrative?

5. An experienced reader can predict the kind of challenges that younger writers might encounter with conventions and mechanics of language as they attempt to write a story. What are some of the challenges you can anticipate, and how can you teach the key concepts in a proactive way?

6. It is hard to agree on the elements that define quality narrative writing, especially since many of the writers we admire are the ones who seem

to break with convention. How can you engage students in a process of defining for themselves what distinguishes a well-written story?

7. It would seem quite natural to link the writing of fiction narrative with the reading of significant works of fiction. How would you link the two activities? What is the advantage to such linkages?

8. How can visual images or other appeals to the senses help students plan and produce fiction narratives?

4

Teaching
Personal Experience
Narratives

A few years ago, Larry Johannessen was helping a high school English department revise its writing curriculum. Examining their current program, he was surprised to discover that most teachers did very little with narrative and descriptive writing. When he asked why, the teachers said students had already done plenty of that in elementary and middle school. Besides, the students needed to prepare for the state writing test, which focused on argumentation, and had to know how to write according to standards expected in college and the real world.

It took quite a bit of discussion to convince these teachers that a good writing curriculum should provide students with a wide variety of writing experiences and that narrative and descriptive writing would help students learn important thinking and writing strategies. Writing about personal experiences is an opportunity for students to think about their own lives.

Task Analysis

The goal of this series of lessons is for students to create a narrative about a significant personal experience that elicits an emotive response from the reader. The narrative should include a variety of descriptive details, along with figurative language and dialogue where appropriate. In other words, the reader will feel what the writer felt and sense vicariously the impact the experience had.

It's tempting to assume that because young people have been exposed to stories their whole lives, they know how to write a detailed, vivid, and engaging personal experience narrative. Being aware of the conventions of constructing a story, however, is insufficient in a structured process approach. Students need to learn *procedures* for generating ideas that might eventually fit the story form and its conventions. We need to do more than simply ask students to recall a significant experience and tell the story compellingly. We need to lead students through a sequence of activities that builds their ability to narrate a personal experience in evocative ways.

Having read many student narratives over the years, we know that most students need considerable help learning how to describe events using appropriate, specific sensory details and how to use figurative language. Most young writers also need help generating ideas to write about. Therefore, instructional activities need to include procedures for learning to write using sensory detail and figurative language. They also need to include social interaction while the students generate ideas and texts so that they receive immediate feedback on their interpretation of the task. Finally, the procedures need to be learned in accessible activities and then applied to more complex tasks.

Stage 1. Assessing What Students Know About Narrative

A preliminary assessment reveals what a particular group of students already knows and doesn't know about personal experience writing. The following prompt will help you find out the extent of your students' prior knowledge about narrative writing:

> Write about an event (a personal experience) and its consequences that had an impact on you or someone you know. Be as specific as you can in describing the event and its consequences or impact. Try to write so that a reader will see what you saw and feel what you felt.

Give students about forty-five minutes to write their compositions.

The responses shown in "Scary Encounter" and "Car Wash" (below) were written by students in the same urban high school—the first by an "at-risk" ninth grader, the second by a "regular" sophomore. While the second composition is longer and contains some specific sensory detail, neither is particularly effective at conveying the experience in ways that engage readers. These student writers need to learn strategies that will enable them to include key sensory and other details and thus convey their experience in more powerful ways.

Personal Experience Essay: "Scary Encounter"

One day my girlfriend, Swaney and me were walking on a highway, when this car came by and tried to hit us, but Swaney saw the car coming and she screamed and pulled me out of the way. Then, the car turned around and started chasing us and both of us started running and we jumped over the guard rail and rolled down the hill. We ran through a tunnel and at the other end the man was standing there waiting for us so we turned around and ran the other way. We saw a man driving a car that we knew and he took us to the police station and they were after the man and captured him. Later we found out that he was an escaped convict from a mental prison.

After that I was so scared I couldn't sleep for a few nights and I had bad nightmares. Now I'm real scared of the same spot where that happened and I'll never go back there again.

Personal Experience Essay: "Car Wash"

It was a warm and sunny day in the spring. Today was a day I've been looking forward to for a month. Our Lady of Good Counsel was having their car wash and I was going to work at it. I hurried and get ready and called my girlfriend Colleen. As I walked out her door I heard the birds singing and dogs barking. I could smell the sweet odor of a new spring day. I saw young kids outside playing ball and jumping rope already. As we neared the school, we could begin to hear explosions of laughter and shouting. We finally got there and cars were already there. I was the cashier and kept all the money in a dented tin box. I got rather bored watching the money so I asked if I could do something else. Then I got sent to the corner store about five times. Soon I just picked up an old torn rag and started washing and drying any car I saw. When we closed, people started squirting each other with the stringy hoses. After a while, everyone was in the act and we had buckets and cups flying. People got thrown in barrels, and someone filled them with soap. Everyone was completely saturated from head to toe. We finally slowed down and sat on the church steps. We counted the money and tried to get a little drier than we were. We all decided to hold a dance with the money we made and finally split up and returned home. We all had a blast that day and even planned another car wash for the future.

Stage 2. Gateway Activity: Promoting Attention to Detail

In the following activity, students pay attention to the specific details of a mundane object—their left shoe—and describe them clearly, vividly, and distinctively enough so that another student can identify the shoe in a big pile of shoes.

Have students take out a sheet of paper and a pen or pencil. Next, in order to match papers to their authors without revealing the students' identities, ask them to number the papers consecutively, one through the number of students in the class. Tell them to make sure both feet are under their desk and out of sight. Without looking, they are to write a detailed description of their left shoe, including as many details as they can remember and being as specific as they can. Someone else in the class should be able to pick out their shoe from a group of similar shoes using their description.

EPISODE 2.1

Patrol the classroom for ten or fifteen minutes as students write their descriptions, making a great show of not allowing students to peek at their left shoe. Collect the compositions as students finish them or when time is up.

Have students put their desks in a circle (or double circle, depending on class size), leaving a space in the middle for a pile of shoes. Give each student a small sticker. Tell them to take off their left shoe, place it on their desk, and affix the sticker to the toe of the sole. Ask two students to collect all the left shoes, number each sticker (using a range of numbers that will not duplicate the numbers the students placed on their compositions), and put them in a pile in the center of the room.

EPISODE 2.2

Once all the shoes are in the center of the room, mix them up into a giant "left-shoe salad." Redistribute the compositions the students wrote so each student gets someone else's. Tell them they are to read the composition they have been given and then see whether they can find the shoe that matches the description. (If someone blurts out, "But so many of them are just alike; how are we going to pick out the right one?" you can teasingly remind them to pick the *left* one, not the right one!) Point out that if their partner has written a good, specific description of the shoe, they should have little difficulty picking the correct one.

EPISODE 2.3

Have students read the compositions silently, looking carefully at the details the writer provided. Then, in groups of four or five, have them look through the shoes for the one that matches the description. When they think they have found the correct shoe, they return to their desk and write the number of the shoe on the composition they were given. (Keep this part of the activity moving along; it should last no more than three or four minutes.)

EPISODE 2.4   Once all the students have had a chance to find a matching shoe, ask volunteers to read their composition while you hold up the shoe they've identified as matching the description. Point out key details that help identify the shoe: prominent scuff marks, discolorations, stains, patterns of wear on the soles, and other identifying characteristics.

Some compositions will offer few if any specific details that help identify the shoe. For example, the student who reads, "It's a white athletic shoe, and it is fairly new. It is a size 9 I think. There is like a black band around the side of the shoe. I think the shoe probably has some scuff marks on it," will probably not be able to pick out the corresponding shoe, since a number of shoes will fit this vague and general description.

EPISODE 2.5   After confirming which shoe corresponds to which description, spend a few minutes discussing why some students found the matching shoe and others did not. Most often the reason is the writer's use of specific details.

If students complain that the activity isn't fair because they were not allowed to look at their left shoe, remind them that when they write about a personal experience, they have to be able to remember specific details related to it, just as you asked them to remember specific details about the shoe they put on their foot that morning and have worn all day. Memory plays an important role in generating specific details that will make a past experience come alive for readers.

Stage 3. Reinforcing the Procedures: A More Complex Descriptive Task

This next activity is a modification of one originally developed by George Hillocks in the early 1970s. We have used it with elementary, middle, and secondary students, as well as with novice writers in college and university composition courses. It's a very effective way to help students learn how to improve their skills in observation and use specific sensory details and figurative language in their descriptions.

Students have begun their descriptive work with shoes, something they presumably know quite well. Now they move on to less familiar objects, in this case seashells (or other handy objects that tend to look more or less the same, such as potatoes, lemons, small decorative stones, carrots, pine cones, figs, apples, black-and-white close-up photographs of insects, photos of tropical fish, decorative buttons, or geodes). The task increases in difficulty as students practice and refine the procedures they learned during the gateway activity. The general structure of Stage 3 is similar to that of Stage 2. What has changed is the complexity of the task.

Beforehand, put together a set of fifteen or sixteen similar seashells or other similar objects. (We usually use small conch shells, each one between three and five inches in length and characterized by brightly colored spirals and a smooth inner surface.) Place a small piece of tape on each shell and number them consecutively. Although all the shells are the same type and have similar colors and spirals, each one is unique in some way. It might be the particular colors or shades of color, the size or exact shape, a chip on one edge, the particular texture, or even the way the spiral is shaped (or misshapen). When students first see the set of shells, they often comment that they all look the same; however, on closer examination, each one is unique.

EPISODE 3.1

Begin by showing a single shell of a different type from the ones you will use later. (We often use a scallop shell.) Hold it up for everyone to see. Point out that if asked to describe it, many people would probably say something like, "It is kind of flat and kind of a half circle shape. It has ridges and it is sort of pink." Then take out a second scallop shell and hold it up next to the original one. "But, as you can see, that description also matches the other shell I just put right next to it. In fact, you probably can't tell which one I was holding first. If you want to describe that shell in such a way that someone would be able to pick it out from another similar shell, you have got to be more specific than I just was."

EPISODE 3.2

Next, offer some details a writer might focus on to distinguish one shell from the other: a difference in exact color or shape or in the particular textures and colors that make up the unique radiating fluted pattern.

Give each group of three or four students one seashell. Ask them to write a group composition (not a list) describing their shell so that another group will be able to pick it out from all the other shells. The opportunity to work with peers throughout the instructional sequence characterizes a structured process approach. In the early stages of a sequence of activities, the peer groups encourage students to talk through their process of describing things in detail; they

EPISODE 3.3

learn through articulating their ideas and also from their classmates' contributions. They also critique one another's ideas, providing immediate feedback and receiving recommendations for how to do their work better. Composing a description as a group enables students to pool their knowledge; later, they will independently apply what they learn to new tasks.

Remind the students that they will probably want to spend some time discussing their shell and taking notes and then write a coherent composition. Give each group a number and tell them to write it at the top of their final composition.

Tell them they may not identify the number taped to their shell or describe the piece of tape; they may not write or make marks on their shell; and they may not drop their shell or in any way cause it to have a distinctive chip or crack that is not already there.

Give them twenty or thirty minutes to write their compositions. While they are working, make a two-column list for yourself aligning the number on each of the shells with the number of the group describing it so you'll know which group has which shell. As students finish their descriptions, collect the shells and the compositions.

EPISODE 3.4 Mix up the shells on a table in front of the classroom (to make the problem more interesting, include any leftover shells), and give each group a composition written by another group. Have the groups read the composition they have been given and, two groups at a time, come to the front of the room, pick the shell they think is being described, write the number of that shell on the composition, and return to their seats.

While the groups are examining shells in the front of the room, ask groups that have already identified their shell, "Do you think you found the right one? What details were most important in helping you pick it out?" If a group seems unsure, ask, "What made it so difficult to find the right shell? What could the writers have done to help you pick it out?" Questions like these keep students focused and prompt them to be more reflective about what is necessary to write an effective description of the shell.

EPISODE 3.5 Once all the groups have had an opportunity to pick out the correct shell, ask each group in turn to read aloud the composition they were given and identify the number of the shell they picked out. The group that wrote the composition then says whether or not this shell is correct.

EPISODE 3.6 When all compositions have been read, assess the results. Usually, about half of the groups will have picked the correct shell. Ask those groups to explain what qualities in the composition enabled them to do so. They will identify specific details that enabled them to distinguish the correct shell from all the others. Point out and emphasize particularly effective specific details. If students have used figurative language, which they often do, reinforce this attribute as well. Hold up the shells so that the entire class can see how the writers used specific sensory details, including figurative language, to differentiate their shell.

Before the groups return their compositions to the writers, ask them to underline the best specific detail, circle one part that was vague or confusing, and write one thing that could be done to improve the composition. This final step encourages students to reflect about what they have learned and practiced.

EPISODE 3.7

You can use this activity—with different objects—more than once. The only requirement is that the objects compel students to observe carefully and translate their observations into specific details in writing.

Depending on the class and how well or poorly students did the first time, you may have them work in pairs instead of small groups during a second go-round. The reduction in group size reduces the level of support. The second round should also provide a greater challenge, requiring them to be more specific.

This sequence of activities helps students understand why it is important to use specific sensory details and figurative language; it also helps them develop some strategies for using clear and vivid description. Students often take on the corrective role teachers are accustomed to assuming. In one ninth-grade class, a boy loudly complained that the students who received his group's composition should have been able to pick out the correct shell. He said that the shell had brown spots and that the description had specified this. A student in the berated group walked up to the front of the room and picked up both the correct shell and the one the group had thought was correct. She walked over to the boy, held both shells up, and said with exasperation, "Yes, it has brown spots [holding out the correct shell], but look, so does this one!" Then she glanced at the table full of shells and said, "They all have brown spots. You have got to be more specific than that." The point was very powerfully made, not only to the boy who complained, but also to the rest of the class.

If students are going to write a successful composition, they must observe their shell or other object closely, note specific details, and include them in their compositions. Those who do not do a very good job see why they need to observe closely and why they need to include specific details in their writing.

Stage 4. Learning Task-Specific Procedures: Helping Students Use a Variety of Sensory Details

Most students need help understanding that good descriptive and narrative writing contains many appropriate sensory details. It also often contains similes and metaphors, and effective dialogue when appropriate, to help make an experience come alive for readers. Chapter 3 describes a series of activities that give students practice in using sight and sound details in their writing and help them learn how to describe a setting and describe action or conflict. Some of the activities in that chapter might be included in this series of activities to help students learn how to describe a personal experience.

You should also include one or more activities to help students learn how to describe events or objects using other sensory details than sight or sound. One particularly effective activity focuses on helping students describe the sense of smell. Our sense of taste is limited to discriminating saltiness, sweetness, sourness, and bitterness. In contrast, the olfactory sense is capable of discriminating more than ten thousand scents. Despite the large number of scents humans can discriminate, the English language is nearly devoid of words to describe smells; this stinks! We have such words as *fruity, resinous, flowery, spicy, putrid*, and *burnt* to describe major categories of smells. Unfortunately, these words, and a few others, such as *rancid, fecund, acrid, fetid, fragrant, sweet*, and *redolent* nearly complete our vocabulary of smells in English. Many odors are simply named by whatever it is that generates them: carnations, the cheesecake factory, the chemistry class, and so on.

Edgar Allan Poe was a master of using sensory details for effect. Yet in "The Pit and the Pendulum" he barely uses the sense of smell, even though his narrator can see virtually nothing. Poe describes two important odors in terms of the substances that give rise to them: "The vapor of heated iron! A suffocating odor," which emanated from the heated walls of the dungeon; and "the peculiar smell of decayed fungus" rising from the pit. His description of smells is limited to a few general adjectives and the naming of particular odoriferous objects.

If Edgar Allan Poe had trouble describing smells, it's likely that students will too. The following activity helps students think of ways to describe smells that go beyond the ordinary. It employs Scratch 'n Sniff stickers, which are available at many supermarkets, office supply stories, drug stores, and teacher stores. They usually come in packs of five to fifteen sheets and are relatively inexpensive. Each sheet has one particular pleasant or malodorous smell: grape, motor oil, strawberry, peanut butter, pizza, mint, and old shoes, among many others. When someone scratches the surface of a sticker, the scent comes through very strongly.

Once you've gathered a variety of Scratch 'n Sniff sheets, the next step is to have students attempt to describe the smells. We recommend doing this activity in small groups so everyone will have the opportunity to talk through how to describe odors. Give each pair or trio of students a "What Is That Smell I Feel?" activity sheet (see Figure 4–1) and a sticker with a different smell (or as many different smells as you can manage in a classroom of twenty-five or thirty students). Go over the directions, emphasizing that the first question asks them to identify the smell. Tell students to scratch their sticker vigorously, because that brings out more of the scent.

EPISODE 4.1

Figure 4–1. What Is That Smell I Feel?

What Is That Smell I Feel?

Name(s) _____ , _____ , _____

1. Identify the substance that you smell:

   _____

2. How does the smell feel? Is it smooth, abrasive, rough? Give at least three words:

   _____

   _____

   _____

3. How does the smell move? Does it creep, surround, push, etc.?

   _____

   _____

4. Compare the smell to something else that will help describe it:

   The smell is like _____

   _____

   (continues)

Figure 4–1. What Is That Smell I Feel? *(continued)*

5. Combine the best details you have written into a sentence that *identifies* the substance and *describes* its smell. Imagine that you have just entered a place and noticed this smell.

    Example: As I opened the door, the rasping stink of the ammonia kicked me in the face.

    _____

    _____

    _____

The first question on the activity sheet focuses their rhinoscular attention on the smell. Questions 2 and 3 ask students to describe each smell in terms of other sensory perceptions, or synaesthesia (using one sense to describe another). Doing so helps them extend their imagination. Question 4 achieves a similar purpose by asking students to compare the smell to something else. Students are now being asked to use similes and metaphors to help them describe the smell. Question 5 prompts students to describe the smell they have been assigned. Since most students have had very little experience writing descriptions of smells, this step helps them turn their observations into written sentences.

It may be a good idea to *model the process* for a class of younger or less experienced students using one Scratch 'n Sniff sticker. Show them how to scratch the sticker to release the strongest aroma; then lead a class discussion of each question. You may encourage further thought by asking additional questions: What color is the smell? What does it make you feel inside? What do you hear when you smell that odor? What does that odor taste like? Encourage a variety of comparisons and list them on the board.

Give students ten or fifteen minutes to complete the "What Is That Smell I Feel?" sheet. As they work, walk around offering guidance, answering questions, and making suggestions.

EPISODE 4.2   Lead a class discussion of the students' answers. Begin by asking students to read aloud the sentence that they wrote for Question 5. Comment on any effective details and figurative language students have used in their culminating sentence to encourage them and reinforce their achievements. (Ask the class to help with any sentences that need improvement.) Once all the sentences have been read, ask for volunteers to read the comparisons they wrote for Question 4, and highlight effective ones. Finally, discuss their answers to Questions 2 and 3. Underscore particularly effective descriptions and discuss why they are distinctive and memorable.

Give students, in pairs or trios or perhaps on their own this time, a second, different Scratch 'n Sniff sticker and a new activity sheet. This step reinforces the skills you introduced students to the first time through.

EPISODE 4.3

Have students extend the strategies they have learned by writing a description of a location where odors are an important part of the experience: different types of ethnic restaurants, a locker room, the school cafeteria, the beach, a kitchen, a candy store, an alley, a bakery, a laundry room, a subway stop, a creek bed, a feed store, a pine forest, factories making specific products (paint, cars, paper products, insect repellants, and so on). Students should write about their impressions of the place, amplified by descriptions of the various odors that fill their nostrils.

EPISODE 4.4

Stage 5. Scaffolding Students' Writing: Generating a Topic

Now that students have spent a number of days learning how to observe closely and describe specific sensory details, including figurative language, they are ready to start writing their personal experience narrative.

Give them the same prompt you used for your preliminary assessment of their writing proficiency:

EPISODE 5.1

> Write about an event (a personal experience) and its consequences that had an impact on you or someone you know. Be as specific as you can in describing the event and its consequences or impact. Try to write so that a reader will see what you saw and feel what you felt.

Repeating this open-ended assignment lets you assess the effects of your instruction by contrasting their original narratives with the ones that they now produce.

If students have trouble finding topics to write about, brainstorm some story ideas. You might think aloud to model generating a list of five or six

ideas, assessing the ideas, and narrowing the possibilities down to one that
meets the criteria for the assignment. Then ask a series of questions to prompt
their thinking and have them generate at least one idea for each question:

1. Remember a time when you felt really happy about something or
   someone. What happened that made you feel so happy?

2. Recall a time when you felt very sad about something or someone.
   What happened that made you feel so sad?

3. Think about the most important person in your life. What happened
   that made you realize how important this person is to you?

4. Remember a time when you experienced an important ritual or event
   that was a critical moment in your life. Why was it so important?

5. Remember a time when you worked hard to accomplish something
   and you were able to do it. What happened? How did you accomplish your goal?

6. Recall an occasion when you worked hard to accomplish or achieve
   something and failed. What happened? How did things go wrong?

7. Think of a time when you were faced with a difficult decision. What
   happened? Did you make the right decision? Why or why not?

8. Recall a time when you had to make an ethical or moral choice.
   What was the choice? Did you do the right thing?

9. Consider an occasion when you had to stand up for yourself or others in the face of danger. How did you act in this situation?

10. Remember a time when you were really frightened or scared. What
    happened? Were you able to overcome your fear? If so, how? If not,
    why not?

EPISODE 5.2   Have students, in pairs or small groups, present their ideas to and get feedback from their partner or fellow group members. They can use the following
questions as a guide:

1. Which idea seems most interesting, exciting, or compelling as the
   basis for a personal experience narrative?

2. Which idea provides the greatest motivation for producing a personal experience narrative told with sensory detail?

3. Are any of the topics inappropriate for school writing?

4. Which idea do you think you or your partner or fellow group member should write about? Why?

You might also ask the pairs or groups to tell the whole class which topics they think would be the best ones to write about and why. This opportunity lets students hear what other students are doing and why. They can then refine their own ideas based on their new perspective.

Stage 6. Generating Task-Specific Evaluative Criteria

Asking students to evaluate stories written by other students before they begin writing their personal experience narratives lets them create a final checklist of what needs to be included. Also, by ranking strong and weak narratives and explaining their reasoning, students develop a sense of discrimination they can apply to their own compositions.

In Chapter 3 generating criteria is a gateway activity; here it occurs later in the sequence. There is no "best" place to include it, but it's a critical part of any writing instruction. In this sequence the detail activities take several days, and generating criteria is more effective if it's done just before the students begin writing. The sequence on fictional narratives in Chapter 3 is briefer, so the criteria could be generated earlier.

Students, in small groups, analyze and discuss the narrative in "The Hit" and the earlier personal narrative examples ("Scary Encounter" and "Car Wash"). They rank the essays from best to worst. ("The Hit" is usually considered the best, "Car Wash" second, and "Scary Encounter" the weakest.) Then they create a list of the qualities or features that distinguish stronger from weaker personal experience narratives.

EPISODE 6.1

Sample Narrative: "The Hit"

As I stepped up to the plate, I could hear the quiet cheers of the crowd in back of me. I laid down my bat on the just swept plate. I could feel my palms begin to sweat as the night air blew a gust of wind past my body. I reached down and picked up some dirt, and as I did, I could feel the heat from the large lights of the ballpark.

I stood up and took a step back from the plate to take a couple of practice swings. My muscles felt tight but began to loosen up as I swung the bat. Finally, the umpire said, "Ok, let's play ball!"

I felt my adrenalin pump through my body. I knew that I had to hit a home run because it was the ninth inning with two outs against us, and we had our worst hitter coming up after me. I laid the bat on my shoulder very gently and took a deep breath while waiting for the pitcher to go into his windup. Finally, the pitcher nodded his head to show he agreed with the signal from the catcher, and he leaned back into his windup. To me he looked almost motionless until he reached forward and released the ball into its swirling orbit. The ball came so fast that it almost caught me off guard. I knew if I waited any longer the ball would go whirling past me, and I would miss a perfect pitch. So I swung the bat around with all my might and hoped that I would make contact. I knew that I really hit the ball because I heard a cracking noise and then I felt a tingling sensation running from my fingers up to my forearm.

At first I could not see the ball in the night sky so I almost thought that I had hit it out of bounds. Yet I heard the crowd cheering so I knew the ball must still be flying in the air. Then I spotted it sailing way up in the sky.

I dropped my bat and ran while at the same time keeping an eye on the ball. I rounded first still running my hardest. Half way to second I dropped my head and put all my might into it because I saw the ball drop right in front of the left fielder's feet. I knew I had to get all the way home. I rounded second. The third base coach signaled for me to stop at third, but I knew that I could make it. I rounded third at full steam, took a wide turn, and headed for home. I saw the catcher getting ready to catch the ball so I took a diving leap, stretching my muscles to touch home plate.

I hit the ground with a thump and began to slide. I could not see anything through all the dust. I reached for the plate and looked up at the umpire. He stood there very still, and then both arms flung to the side as he called me "Safe!"

EPISODE 6.2   Lead a class discussion of group findings and list the features of a high-quality personal experience narrative on the board. Typical features include:

1. The personal experience is sharply focused with a strong impact—the details all work to create an overall impression.

2. It contains a variety of specific, concrete sensory details, including figurative language (simile, metaphor, personification, etc.).

3. It effectively uses dialogue when appropriate.

4. The details and dialogue contribute to the overall impression; the writer has selected and arranged details for effect.

5. The writer uses sentence structure, word choice, vocabulary, usage, and other aspects of language that are suitable for the narrator and situation.

If additional work seems appropriate, have small groups come up with ideas for improving "Car Wash" and lead a class discussion of those ideas. Students might also revise "Car Wash" in small groups or on their own.

EPISODE 6.3

Stage 7. Language Lesson: Playing with Participial Phrases

A minilesson on sentence structure helps students make their narratives more vivid and consciously vary their syntax when they relate events. Recognizing and using introductory participial phrases is one useful structure. (You may see other possibilities that are more appropriate for your students.)

Define what a participial phrase is. A *participle* is a form of a verb that, for regular verbs, ends in *-ing* or *-ed*. Take the verb whose infinitive form is *to cook*. Here are the *present participial* and *past participial* forms of *to cook*. Note that each participle includes a helping verb (*am cooking, have cooked*).

EPISODE 7.1

Present participial form, ending in -ing: I *am cooking* a casserole for dinner.
Past participial form, ending in -ed: I *have cooked* a casserole for dinner.

Each of these verb forms can also be a modifier, often appearing as the first word in an adjective phrase that describes the subject of a sentence. Note that when used as a modifier, the participle does not include the helping verb. Here is an example of each:

Present participial phrase: *Cooking all day*, I prepared a lovely meal.
Past participial phrase: *Cooked for two hours*, the noodles were most soggy.

Participial phrases are an interesting means by which to vary sentence structure. They can also create comical sentences when they are intended to modify one noun but instead modify another. Here's a memorable sentence written by one of our students: "Crashing into the rocks, the gulls flew above the waves." The participial phrase is *crashing into the rocks*. Presumably, the author meant to indicate that the waves were crashing into the rocks as the gulls flew overhead. But as written, the sentence says that the gulls were crashing into the rocks. Oy.

To help students construct sentences that open with a participial phrase, give them sets of brief sentences that they combine into one sentence in which the opening phrase begins with a present or past participle. Here are two brief sentences that could be combined into one, with one converted into a participial phrase:

> *Todd drove home from work one day.*
> *Todd saw something he had never seen before.*

Ask, "What is the present participial form of *drove*?" If students don't say *driving*, follow up with, "How could you take the first sentence and make it into a participial phrase that modifies the second sentence?" Ultimately, you should arrive at something resembling, *Driving home from work one day, Todd saw something he had never seen before.* Model the same process using a past participial phrase to combine these sentences: *I was blinded by the light. I didn't see the train coming.*

To prompt students to think about how participial structures work in sentences, particularly how easily they can modify an unintended noun, introduce an exercise like the one in Figure 4–2.

Figure 4–2. Participial Phrase or Dangling Participle?

The following sentences open with either a past or present participial phrase. Each modifies a noun in the main clause of the sentence. Work with a partner to tell which noun it modifies, and then decide whether it modifies the noun that the author intended or not. Rewrite any sentence in which you think that the phrase modifies the wrong noun.

1. Blasted by the dynamite, the coal miners opened up a new mine shaft in the mountain.

2. Coming around the corner, I saw my path blocked by a dumpster on the sidewalk.

3. Forgotten by everyone, poor little Joey was left behind at the museum during the field trip.

4. Stuffing food into my mouth, my mother told me to hurry up and finish my dinner.

5. Believing that crime does not pay, the judge ordered the ice cream truck thief to spend the rest of his life in jail.

(continues)

Figure 4–2. Participial Phrase or Dangling Participle? *(continued)*

6. Blown over by the tornado, the townspeople rebuilt the court house.

7. Buried under five feet of snow, we used shovels to uncover my car.

8. Throwing right-handed, Lefty McDougle's spear landed right next to the bull's-eye.

9. Piled high on my desk, the papers made it hard for me to work.

10. Taking an extra fifty dollars, the bank was unaware of my large withdrawal.

Students are now ready to combine pairs of sentences into one sentence that opens with a participial phrase. It doesn't matter whether it's a past or present participle, as long as the phrase modifies the intended noun. One such exercise is provided in Figure 4–3.

EPISODE 7.4

Figure 4–3. Sentence Combining—Participial Phrases

Each item in this exercise contains two sentences. Combine them into one sentence that opens with either a past or present participial phrase. Make sure that the phrase modifies the word that you intend it to describe.

1. Bigby Hinds was getting hungry.

   Bigby decided to grab a bite to eat.

2. Bigby walked down the street.

   Bigby was looking for a restaurant.

3. Dinah Thirst was late for work at the onion processing plant.

   Dinah was driving a bit too fast.

4. Dinah saw Bigby walking down the sidewalk.

   Dinah wondered why Bigby didn't appear to have a job.

(continues)

Figure 4–3. Sentence Combining—Participial Phrases *(continued)*

5. Bigby was getting hungrier by the moment.

   Bigby caught a whiff of Dinah's onion-scented car.

6. Bigby was plagued by a recent operation to his nasal passages.

   Bigby couldn't tell the difference between Dinah's car and an onion burger.

7. Dinah swerved to avoid a possum.

   Dinah turned the wheel of her car frantically.

8. Bigby strongly resembled a possum.

   Bigby didn't smell so good either.

9. Bigby smelled neither good nor well.

   Bigby was considering getting a rhinoscopy and taking a shower.

10. Dinah thought this was a splendid idea.

    Dinah drove more carefully to the onion processing plant with a clothespin on her nose.

Stage 8. From Group to Individual: Drafting the Narratives

Students produce a draft of their personal experience narratives. You decide whether they write in class or at home and how long before the writing is due.

Stage 9. From Individual to Group: Peer Response to Drafts

Students now revise their drafts. In the approach to working with rough drafts described in Chapter 3, students meet in pairs and read their stories aloud to their partners; each partner identifies a favorite part and possible omissions in the other's narrative; and each partner copyedits the other's paper for problems with usage, punctuation, and spelling.

Another way to handle revision is to have students meet in small groups of three or four and use the features of a successful personal experience essay they generated in class to evaluate each composition and suggest revisions. Each student reads his or her essay aloud, and the other members of the group use the checklist criteria to determine if and how well the essay fits each of the features.

Ask the groups to do the following for each composition:

EPISODE 9.1

1. Tell the writer one thing that he or she did well in the essay. What is the most effective feature or aspect of the essay?

2. Tell the writer one thing that could be improved in the essay. What feature is missing or weak in the essay?

3. Suggest how the writer could improve the missing or weak part of the essay. What is one thing the writer could do to improve the missing or weak part?

Each student in the group then reads the other group members' essays silently and marks any errors in spelling, punctuation, and grammar for possible correction.

Have the students, in small groups, read their finished essays aloud. You might also have each group select one personal experience essay to read aloud to the class.

EPISODE 9.2

Extensions

1. Have students, in small groups, dramatize one narrative (or a combination of narratives) and perform it for the class. (This performance could be a conventional skit, a filmed short play, a storyboard, an animated short feature, or whatever else they come up with.)

2. Have students write personal experience narratives that relate to the themes they are studying in literature: coming of age, responsibility, adolescent relationships, conflict with authority, etc. (see Smagorinsky 2008).

3. Have students work through various parts of the process on their blogs. This more public presentation lets students move their writing outside the classroom into social spaces in which they have a different kind of investment.

What Makes This Sequence a Structured Process Approach?

This sequence of activities focuses on specific strategies that enable writers to embellish their personal experience narratives by paying attention to detail, using descriptive language, and employing similes and metaphors. These strategies are not exclusive to personal experience narratives—these activities could be included in any sequence in which the writer benefits from including detail. However, the strategies do enhance the telling of personal experiences in ways that make them task-specific, if not task-exclusive.

Collecting seashells (or buying figs, finding pictures of insects or fish on the Internet, etc.) and designing minilessons and exercises need to be done ahead of time, outside class. What happens in class, however, is primarily the province of the students as they describe shoes and like objects, critique one another's descriptions, generate criteria to guide their writing, and draft and revise their narratives.

One benefit of this approach is that instruction rarely gets tedious or repetitive. While the routines might recur, what happens within them is different in every class. Presenting the same sequence of activities in three different classes does not yield the same script each time but rather produces different interactions, descriptions, insights, and realizations. The teaching day is therefore filled with more energy, greater variation, and increased appreciation of students as they demonstrate abilities that might be masked or forced underground in a more teacher-dominated classroom.

The impetus for generating procedures and evaluative criteria is largely in the students' hands, under your guidance. Students thus have a better chance at internalizing both; actively generating them and reinforcing them through interaction, students are more likely to own the process and the outcome of their work.

The instruction moves from readily accessible and easily knowable material—the students' own shoes—through increasingly difficult tasks such as differentiating shells and potatoes. With these descriptive strategies in place, students then move on to the highly social process of considering their own experiences and the details that make telling about them a more empathic and visceral experience for their readers. These readers are immediate, providing feedback and suggestions while ideas are generated and drafts are produced and revised. The readership for students' writing is expanded beyond the teacher, who becomes less a strict examiner and more a member of a larger community of readers.

You are still "the decider" when it comes to grades (unless student grading is woven into the sequence), but the criteria for evaluation are generated by the students through their inductive ranking of sample stories. These sample stories are not "model" stories to emulate, but rather compositions that students scrutinize in order to identify the qualities that may be present in one story and absent in another. The students are then responsible for making their own determinations about what they value in writing, what qualities they will include in their personal experience narratives, and which criteria they will be evaluated against.

The language lesson on participial phrases is pointed, relatively brief, and directly tied to a quality that could come into play in the writing of personal experience narratives. Using participial phrases benefits the writer in virtually any sort of written composition, but doing so is a particularly valuable way to vary the syntax in a personal experience narrative. Rather than being conducted in isolation, language study is thus incorporated into the students' need for clear written expression and communication.

These lessons scaffold students' progress through a sequence of activities in which they are taught specific procedures and strategies for producing a personal experience narrative. Students receive support from both you and their peers at each stage of the process, and you monitor their learning and determine whether or not additional activities are necessary before moving forward. Your judgment is an important factor throughout the instruction, but the students are active participants in the classroom. Through careful design and preparation—and wise consideration of the degree to which students have grasped procedures for producing the qualities of personal experience narratives—you play a critical, if at times hidden, role in the students' development as writers.

Questions for Reflection

1. Are there any topics that would be "off limits" to your student writers in their production of personal narratives? If so, which ones, and why? How will you monitor their topic selection so that it is appropriate for school?

2. As you teach students how to write in greater detail, are there occasions when they should learn about level of detail in relation to the pacing of the story? That is, can excessive details derail the story's momentum? If so, how do you address this problem instructionally?

3. How do you teach students how to balance their inclusion of descriptive adjectives with their need to avoid overdoing such descriptions?

4. What steps would you take if a student's personal narrative included information that you consider dangerous or unhealthy for the student or others?

5. To what degree would you encourage or discourage personal narrative writing that includes phrasing in non-English languages, especially when written by students from immigrant families?

6. How can the use of technology enhance students' production of personal narrative writing?

7. Is it appropriate to enhance personal narrative writing with the inclusion of other genres such as art, music, and so forth? Why or why not?

8. How can personal narrative writing instruction be incorporated into the language and literature curricula for different grade levels?

9. How can personal narrative writing instruction address the demands of testing mandates?

10. How do you know when a student has written a "good" personal narrative, including the quality of the topic, the story arc, the characters, and other factors?

5

Teaching Argumentation Essays

In his study of state writing assessments, Hillocks (2002) finds that teachers often feel great pressure to increase students' scores. He reports that some teachers encourage their students to fabricate the evidence they offer as support for their generalizations when they know little about the topic specified in the prompt. To a certain extent we understand: these teachers are no doubt skeptical about the value of the state assessments. Because the writing only matters in the context of the assessment, they distinguish students' writing for the test from other occasions when they would expect the writer to make an honest effort to advance the reader's understanding of the topic.

Hillocks finds that the standard for judging writing on state assessments is expressed in two ways: the rubric that guides the raters and the examples the state offers to illustrate the elements in the rubric. He also notes that in many states the scoring rubric and the illustrative examples are geared to the five-paragraph theme (Hillocks 2005). Johnson et al. (2003) identify the pressures and historical lineage that lead to the five-paragraph theme's stubborn presence in schools. In much five-paragraph-theme instruction, proficiency is achieved by erecting an organizational skeleton and fleshing it out with verbiage—often, in Hillocks' view, "blether" rather than ideas of any value (2005, 80). Hillocks argues that the emphasis on form undervalues the importance of teaching the thinking processes that help writers generate reasonable and substantive texts.

Argument is an element in various kinds of writing: reports, exposition, persuasion, analysis, thesis papers, and so forth. Influenced by Toulmin (1958) and Toulmin et al. (1984), we define *argument* as thinking presented by way of a claim, grounds (i.e., data, examples, or evidence), warrants, backing, rebuttal, and response. In order to produce mature arguments, a writer needs to be able to think clearly and write logically according to the social conventions for persuading others of an opinion. Even so, students as young as fourth graders have the knowledge to be able to make argumentative points (McCann 1989).

Task Analysis

The instructional sequence in this chapter teaches students procedures that will enable them to construct arguments in both current and future writing. It begins with relatively simple arguments and moves toward more complex ones that require students to build on their initial efforts and take into account opposing views. The lessons depicted in this chapter were enacted by three different teachers who all followed a common curriculum.

Ms. Fischer, the teacher in whose classroom the sequence is introduced, begins her lesson planning early in the school year, knowing that by the spring, her fifth graders should be able to write relatively mature essays. Envisioning the texts she wants students to be able to produce, she recognizes that they will need to be able to link units of thought in a coherent and organized way and are going to need help doing so. Approximately one quarter of the students come from low-income homes. Eight are English language learners. Ms. Fischer's instruction has to bridge the many ways of thinking and speaking represented in the class.

Ms. Fischer's goal for the initial lesson, which will introduce students to writing arguments, is for all students to be able to:

- Examine a body of information and draw logical conclusions about trends and patterns.

- Write a coherent and logical paragraph that expresses a claim and supports the claim by citing relevant data and interpreting this data.

Ms. Fischer will also use these two components of her goal as the evaluation criteria when she provides feedback on the students' compositions.

Ms. Fischer gauges her learners' readiness for the lessons by assessing the writing they have done for her so far this year and by talking with their fourth-grade teachers. The students have done little persuasive writing; their writing instruction through fourth grade has focused on relating personal experiences and gathering and summarizing information, types of writing often stressed in early primary school (Graves 1989, 2003). Ms. Fischer therefore assumes that while students may often argue, they have little formal knowledge of argument.

Ms. Fischer also designs specific learning activities that will help her students learn how to make claims, support claims with credible grounds, warrant the evidence, and anticipate and rebut opposing points of view. She is guided by two questions: *What kind of problem will the fifth graders care about? What kind of data will support their thinking about the problem?*

She also wants the activities to engage students in thinking processes and purposeful interaction. She wants students to gather data and use it as the basis for making claims. But since she *doesn't* want gathering data to be time-consuming or cumbersome, she needs to make the information easily accessible, in terms of both acquiring it and making sense of it. She decides the students' own beliefs comprise a good, convenient, accessible, and comprehensible data set and devises a way to elicit those beliefs and make them readily available using the following materials:

- Plain yellow three-by-three-inch sticky notes.

- Fluorescent three-by-three-inch sticky notes.

- Eighteen-by-twenty-four-inch chart paper, each sheet labeled with a category: Music/Dance, Shopping, Sports, Socializing, Time with Family, TV/Movies, Computers and Video Games, Reading, and Gardening.

Stage 1. Gateway Activity: Learning Procedures for Making Evidence-Based Claims

Ms. Fischer tells her students, "I want to get to know all of you as quickly as possible. I know that I don't have time to go around the room and interview everyone, so I have figured out a method to get a basic sense of who you are. I especially want to know about the activities you find the most fun or engrossing." She then models the process by reviewing some of her many interests, distinguishing between activities she finds pleasant and nice and those she finds totally engrossing (e.g., watching her favorite programs on

EPISODE 1.1

television or walking her Maltese dog are pleasant activities, but reading a good book, playing tennis, or talking to an old friend on the phone can be totally engrossing).

EPISODE 1.2   Ms. Fischer then distributes the sticky note pads and says: "On plain yellow sticky notes, briefly describe activities that interest you, one idea per note. On the brightly colored sticky notes, describe activities you find totally engrossing—experiences in which you become so deeply involved that you lose all track of time." After a few minutes, groups of students talk about the things they like to do. After ten more minutes, most desks are filled with sticky notes.

EPISODE 1.3   Ms. Fischer asks the students to stop writing and collects the unused sticky pads. Students, at their desks, organize their sticky notes into categories according to the labels at the top of chart paper posted around the room: Music/Dance, Shopping, Sports, Socializing, Time with Family, TV/Movies, Computers and Video Games, Reading, and Gardening. Then, group by group, they stick their notes under the appropriate categories on the chart paper (see the photos in Figures 5–1, 5–2, and 5–3). This activity takes approximately fifteen minutes.

Figure 5–1.
Students
Using Sticky
Notes to
Collect Data

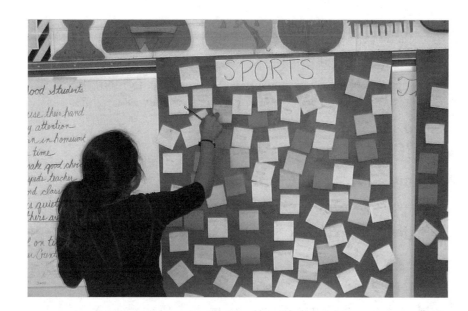

Figure 5–2.
Student
Tallying
Data About
Students'
Interests

Figure 5–3.
Student
Comparing
Information
About
Students'
Interests

Ms. Fischer asks, "What do fifth graders especially enjoy doing?" She emphasizes they must move beyond what they *personally* enjoy and consider the patterns revealed on the chart paper.

Ms. Fischer: Based on what you see around the room [on the chart paper], what would you say fifth graders especially like to do?

Bethany: Students really like sports.

Ms. Fischer: Why would you say that?

Bethany: Look at all of the sticky notes.

Ms. Fischer: What do you mean?

Bethany: There are a lot of sticky notes on the sheet that says Sports.

Ms. Fischer: So what?

Carson: There are probably more there than anywhere else.

Ms. Fischer: So you would say that sports is the highest-ranking choice?

Carson: That's right.

Ms. Fischer: Then what would you say that students are far less interested in doing?

Katrina: They don't really like gardening.

Ms. Fischer: How do you know?

Katrina: There are only four sticky notes there.

Ms. Fischer: So what does that mean?

Katrina: If it was popular, there would be a lot of notes.

The students count the sticky notes under each category and determine the total number overall. These numerical data are additional information on which to base their judgments. Class members continue to identify the most popular and least popular activities based on the data.

Ms. Fischer: How do you know that the fifth graders especially like sports?

Araceli: Look at all of the sticky notes.

Ms. Fischer: What do you mean?

Araceli: There are like a million notes under Sports.

Ms. Fischer: A million? How many, exactly?

Freddy: There were eighty-eight votes.

Ms. Fischer: Since there were four hundred total votes, we calculated that to be 22 percent. What does that show?

Stephania: That 22 percent of our class likes sports.

Ms. Fischer: Is that true? Let's see. How many of you like sports? [*All hands go up.*] Look at that. Everyone likes sports: that's 100 percent. So you can't say that only 22 percent of the class likes sports. What does that number mean?

Freddy: That 22 percent of all the votes were for sports.

Ms. Fischer: That sounds more accurate—that 22 percent of all of our votes went on the big sheet of paper labeled Sports. But that doesn't sound like a lot.

Colleen: Yeah, but compared to gardening or reading, it really is a lot.

Ms. Fischer: So you are saying that while the 22 percent might seem small, it is really the largest percentage of our votes. Is that right?

Colleen: You got it.

By guiding their thinking, Ms. Fischer helps the students look beneath the surface of their initial impressions, taking them through a process of warranting claims and data—that is, explaining why a specific example serves as evidence of a claim.

Ms. Fischer decides to make the process of warranting explicit so that students will use it when they produce their arguments. She develops the worksheet in Figure 5–4 to help students focus deliberately on the development of warrants to tie together their claims and data.

EPISODE 1.5

Ms. Fischer next asks the students to write a paragraph stating a conclusion based on their interpretation of the data and supporting this conclusion with the relevant information. Before they begin, she thinks out loud as she composes a sample paragraph (on a projected transparency) in which she transforms data about teachers into evidence. Here is what she says as she writes:

EPISODE 1.6

Ms. Fischer: I talked recently to all of the teachers at our school about their plans for the weekend. I discovered that many of the teachers like gardening. You might wonder how I figured this out. Here is how I know.

Figure 5–4. Warranting Evidence

A *warrant* is a statement that explains why a particular *example* provides evidence that supports a particular *claim*. Often, a warrant is introduced by words that mean the same thing as *because*. These words and phrases include:

due to	owing to
in light of	since
in that	through
in view of the fact that	whereas
inasmuch as	

Let's say, for instance, that you make the following claim:

> Fifth graders like sports more than any other activity.

You then back up this claim with the following data:

> A survey showed that 22 percent of all students at Conrad Elementary School identify sports as their favorite activity.

Because 22 percent appears to be a small percentage of students, you need to explain *why* the data provide evidence for the claim, in the form of a *warrant*. The following warrant explains why the example supports the claim:

> *Due to* the fact that 22 percent was the highest percentage named for any activity, it is therefore the students' favorite.

Here are a few more illustrations of a claim, data, and supporting warrant:

Claim: Labrador retrievers are a more popular pet than any other dog.
Data: According to the American Kennel Club, the Labrador retriever was the most commonly registered dog in the U.S. in 1997, 2002, 2006, and 2007.
Warrant: *Because* year after year the Labrador retriever has been bought as a new pet more than any other dog, this breed is more popular than any other.

Claim: Rottweilers are not as popular as they used to be.
Data: In 1997 they were the second most often registered dog; in 2007 they were the fifteenth most often registered dog.
Warrant: *In that* they were not bought as often as they were in 1997 compared with other breeds of dog, Rottweilers declined in popularity in the decade between 1997–2007.

(continues)

Figure 5–4. Warranting Evidence *(continued)*

> **Claim:** Cocker spaniels are more popular pets than Sussex spaniels.
>
> **Data:** Cocker spaniels have been among the top twenty newly registered dog breeds in every year between 1997–2007, while Sussex spaniels have never finished higher than 136.
>
> **Warrant:** *Since* cocker spaniels are consistently among the favorite breed of dogs among the 157 listed by the American Kennel Club, and Sussex spaniels are always ranked near the bottom, it's safe to conclude that cocker spaniels are more popular pets.

The following exercise is a series of claims followed by data. Write a warrant, using the words in the lists above, to explain why the data support the claim. Alternatively, if you disagree that the evidence supports the claim, rewrite the claim and then provide a warrant that explains why the evidence now supports it.

1. **Claim:** Michael Jackson's album *Thriller* is the most popular music ever recorded.
   Data: It has sold over 100 million copies, more than twice as many as any album in history.
   Warrant:

2. **Claim:** It's going to rain soon.
   Data: Dark clouds are overhead and I see lightning on the horizon.
   Warrant:

3. **Claim:** Bowling is America's favorite sport.
   Data: More people bowl than participate in any other sport.
   Warrant:

4. **Claim:** People keep getting taller with each generation.
   Data: In the National Basketball Association, the average height of players was 6'4" in 1950, 6'5.5" in 1960, 6'6" in 1970, 6'6.5" in 1980, 6'7" in 1990, and 6'7.5" in 2000.
   Warrant:

5. **Claim:** Breakfast Chocolate Chunks are sweeter than Oat Loops.
   Data: Breakfast Chocolate Chunks are 53 percent sugar; Oat Loops are only 45 percent sugar.
   Warrant:

6. **Claim:** Vegetarians should not eat gelatin.
   Data: Gelatin is made from the boiled bones, hooves, skins, and tendons of animals.
   Warrant:

(continues)

Figure 5–4. Warranting Evidence *(continued)*

7. **Claim:** Missouri is west of Kentucky.
   Data: Missouri is west of the Mississippi River, and Kentucky is east of it.
   Warrant:

8. **Claim:** Conrad Elementary School students are the best readers in the state.
   Data: Conrad School's reading scores are the highest in the state.
   Warrant:

9. **Claim:** Blue jays are mean and aggressive birds.
   Data: They have a reputation for stealing eggs and chicks from other birds' nests, and more than 1 percent of blue jay carcasses show evidence of other birds' eggs and body parts in their stomachs.
   Warrant:

10. **Claim:** The rose is a beautiful but dangerous plant.
    Data: Its stem has thorns that may rip deep gashes in a person's flesh.
    Warrant:

They talked about a lot of plans, but sixteen of the twenty-six teachers said they planned to do some gardening. That's more than half of the teachers. Someone might say, "So what?" The next most popular activity was shopping, with ten of the twenty-six teachers saying they planned to shop over the weekend. I have to conclude that gardening is a very popular activity among teachers at Conrad School, because more than half of the teachers chose to garden over the weekend. The teachers chose gardening more often than any other activity.

Here's the paragraph she wrote based on this thinking process:

When I asked the teachers at our school about their plans for the weekend, sixteen of the twenty-six teachers said they planned to do some gardening. The next most popular activity was shopping, with ten of the twenty-six teachers saying they planned to shop over the weekend. I conclude that gardening is a very popular activity among teachers at Conrad School, because more than half of the teachers chose to garden over the weekend. The teachers chose gardening more often than any other activity.

Ms. Fischer has modeled a *process* for converting raw information to analyzed data to a written opinion based on the data.

Each student composes a draft of a paragraph as Ms. Fischer monitors their attempts and provides assistance as needed. The following samples illustrate the kind of paragraphs the students produced.

EPISODE 1.7

> Out of all the fifth graders at Conrad School, they liked sports the best. The survey we did showed that 88 out of 400 votes were for sports. That may not seem like much, but gardening only got 2 votes. The other categories got around 12 to 53 votes. Compared to the others, 88 votes for sports looks much bigger.
>
> —Emily

> The fifth grade students at Conrad School like to play sports. In a recent survey of fifth graders, 22% of the total votes was for sports. That's high because the ones that have fewer than 88 votes in the survey will be lower than 22%. All of the other ones are less than 88 votes. This result shows that fifth grade kids like to play sports.
>
> —Ryan

> The students in Ms. Fischer's class really like to play sports. In a recent survey, 88 votes were for sports, out of 400 total. This is a lot more than other categories, which many of them only got 20 or lower votes. The result of this survey showed that majority of the fifth graders enjoy playing sports.
>
> —Sawyer

> The students at Conrad School in fifth grade really like sports and social activities. Some popular sports are baseball, softball, and soccer. Some popular socializing is playing with friends. I know all of this from a recent survey with notes. There were 88 entries for sports and 53 entries for socializing. This survey shows the top two popular entries answered by real kids. So there is proof that out of 400 entries, 53 of them were for socializing and 88 of them were for sports.
>
> —Kaeli

When the students complete their drafts, Ms. Fischer calls on volunteers to read their paragraphs aloud. After listening to each example, Ms. Fischer and some of the students comment on the extent to which the paragraph follows the model for reasoning:

EPISODE 1.8

- The writer made a claim.

- The writer supported the claim by citing data.

- The writer explained the meaning or significance of the data and how the data served as evidence supporting the claim.

Students, in pairs, exchange papers and peer edit, concentrating on two sets of considerations. First, they check to see whether the writer has made a claim, supported it with data, and explained the meaning of the data so that it serves as convincing evidence; they also judge whether or not the author's reasoning is logical. Then they check matters of form, including spelling, punctuation, capitalization, and complete sentences. This review takes approximately ten minutes.

Each writer revises her or his paragraph using the peer editor's comments.

Stage 2. Learning Procedures for Arguing in Favor of a Choice

The getting-to-know-you activity has revealed that writers often have difficulty interpreting the data they offer as support for their claims. It is obvious to the fifth graders which activity is most popular. They can look at the charts posted around the room and see immediately which category has the most votes. It's easy to assume that any reasonable reader will draw the same conclusion. Why is it necessary to interpret the evidence?

But during the class discussion the students confuse the percentage of votes cast for sports with the percentage of students who actually like sports. Evidence is not always self-explanatory. These students need rules for interpretation—which can change from context to context—in order to be able to work with the data. Ms. Fischer discusses this challenge with Ms. Alleman, a colleague at nearby Gotha School.

Ms. Fischer and Ms. Alleman want to present their learners with a problem they care about, a problem in which the students devise the rules they will rely on as they examine the data sets and interpret the significance of certain features or attributes. Their experience tells them that fifth graders find visual data most appealing.

Ms. Alleman develops and presents a series of lessons to her class, which is not as diverse as Ms. Fischer's but does include English language learners and three students who have significant learning challenges. Here are Ms. Alleman's goals:

- All students will develop procedures for informal reasoning.

- All students will apply the procedures for informal reasoning when analyzing data and drawing logical conclusions.

- All students will apply the procedures for informal reasoning in a written analysis of a problem in which they apply a set of criteria while judging the relative merits of proposed school mascots/team names.

The materials Ms. Alleman uses are examples of unconventional school mascots/team names—Banana Slugs, Pretzels, Wooden Shoes, and Alices—and depictions of submissions for a proposed mascot for an elementary school.

Ms. Alleman introduces the activity by noting that school mascots identify and distinguish a school and a community. Students, staff, and graduates take pride in the school mascot. She asks the students to share their impressions and feelings about their own school mascot (the common field mouse) and the associations it conjures up. These questions prompt the discussion:

EPISODE 2.1

- What is our school mascot?

- How was the mascot selected?

- Do you like the mascot? Why or why not?

- If you were to select a different mascot, what would it be? Why would you select it?

The students evaluate the school's choice of mascot, and some are adamant that it be changed.

To help the students articulate criteria for a good school mascot, Ms. Alleman displays four mascots of real sports teams on an overhead transparency (see Figure 5–5): the University of California Santa Cruz Banana Slug, the Freeport (IL) High School Pretzel, the Teutopolis (IL) High School Wooden Shoe, and the Vincennes Lincoln (IN) High School Alice ("Big A"). She asks the students to evaluate the merits of each mascot:

EPISODE 2.2

- Do you think the mascot is a good one?

- If you like it, what makes it a good mascot?

- If you don't like it, what makes it a bad mascot?

Initially, the students dismiss the mascots as "stupid" or "dumb." When pressed to explain what makes a mascot dumb, one student observes that pretzels are not something she would take pride in. She adds that they don't suggest a fierce opponent in competitive events, which gets at the heart of a mascot's purpose.

Figure 5–5. Mascots of Real Schools

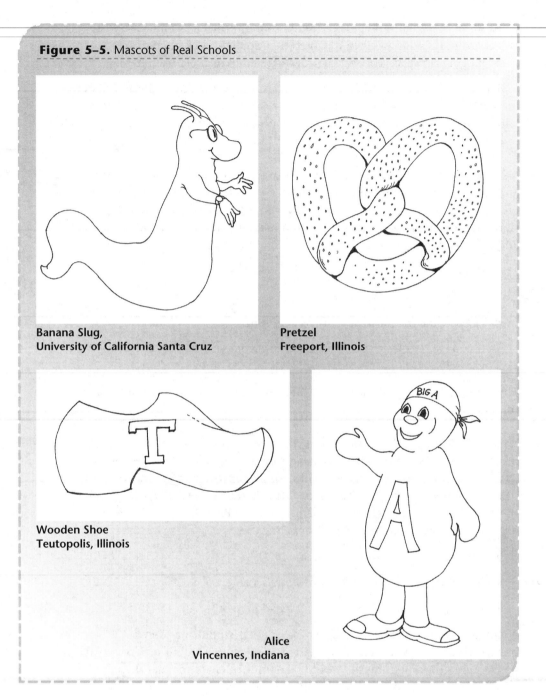

Banana Slug,
University of California Santa Cruz

Pretzel
Freeport, Illinois

Wooden Shoe
Teutopolis, Illinois

Alice
Vincennes, Indiana

Next Ms. Alleman divides the class into groups of three or four and asks each group to propose four or five evaluation criteria for selecting a mascot/team name for a brand new school. Ms. Alleman then moves from group to group, checking their progress and paraphrasing some of their ideas. For example:

Jacqui: What about big?

Mary Jane: Maybe like slugs—could be funny?

Carl: Sure!

Mary Jane: Needs to be unusual; stands out.

Jimmy: Interesting.

Carl: It could also be unique.

Mary Jane: Well, that's the same as stands out.

Jacqui: Maybe stands out is too hard.

Jimmy: Intimidating.

Carl: Yeah, that's a good one.

Jimmy: Proud.

Mary Jane: Has to have something to do with the school.

Carl: Representing it!

Jacqui: Large instead of tiny.

Mary Jane: No! Think about the slugs. They aren't big.

Jacqui: Think about the Dukes [the mascot for the local high school].

Carl: We all like the Dukes!

Jacqui: Strong. We like that!

Jimmy: Powerful.

Mary Ann: That's like strong.

Jacqui: What's our school color?

Jimmy: Blue and grey.

Jacqui: Okay, has something to do with the color.

To prompt the students to consider a broad range of criteria, Ms. Alleman calls on representatives from each group to report what they have come up with. As they paraphrase, clarify, and evaluate all the suggestions, the class derives a common set of criteria for a good mascot/team name. Ms. Alleman records the criteria on an overhead transparency and asks all the students to copy the final version:

- Good mascots/team names are often strong or tough or fierce animals (e.g., Detroit Lions, University of Georgia Bulldogs, University of Kentucky Wildcats, University of Wisconsin Badgers).

- Some good mascots/team names are cuddly, such as the Fort Collins (CO) High School Lambkins and the Omaha Benson (NE) High School Bunnies.

- Good mascots/team names often have some connection to the school, community, or state, especially when the name is unique (e.g., Joliet Ironmen, Purdue Boilermakers, Texas Christian University Horned Frogs, Green Bay Packers, Cobden Appleknockers, Nebraska Cornhuskers, Savannah Sand Gnats, Oklahoma Sooners).

- Good mascots/team names are usually something that someone would be proud to be (e.g., University of Washington Huskies, Vanderbilt University Commodores, Rutgers University Scarlet Knights, Kenyon College Lords).

- The mascot/team name should be appropriate for both boys and girls, unless the boys' and girls' teams go by different names (e.g., the Stephen F. Austin University Lumberjacks/Ladyjacks).

- A good mascot/team name is usually something that community members and students can relate to; names like the Yuma (AZ) High School Criminals are rare, while the name of the Chinook (MT) High School Sugar Beeters shows pride in a community industry.

- Good mascots/team names often use alliteration or assonance so they will sound right when linked with the school name (e.g., Leo (IN) High School Lions, Mesquite (TX) High School Skeeters, Richmond (NC) High School Raiders).

- Some good mascots/team names rely on inside jokes, such as the University of California Irvine Anteaters and the Williams College Purple Cow.

- Good mascots/team names may be funny or rely on puns, as in the Macon Whoopee (minor league hockey team), the Poca (WV) High

School Dots, the Gwinnett Gwizzlies (minor league basketball team), and others.

- Although mascots/team names in the past were often related to Native American tribes, today such names are viewed as controversial or offensive and should be avoided (e.g., Wynnewood (OK) High School Savages, Cleveland Indians, Illinois Fighting Illini), even when they appear to focus on strong attributes (e.g., Atlanta Braves).

To give her students practice in applying these criteria, Ms. Alleman asks them to imagine that the John L. Lewis Elementary School has just opened but has not selected a mascot. The assignment (see Figure 5–6) centers on the proposed mascots depicted in Figure 5–7.

EPISODE 2.4

Figure 5–6. Mascot Problem

The John L. Lewis Elementary School leaders are running a contest to select the new mascot for the school. The image of the mascot will appear on the gym floor, on school stationery, on school-spirit clothing, and on publications. Four drawings (attached) have been selected for final consideration, and you are one of the judges. Here is what you need to do:

Evaluate each of the drawings, and write an explanation of why it would or would not serve as a good mascot, based on the evaluation criteria the class has developed together.

In making a judgment, keep the evaluation criteria in mind, consider the profile of the school and community (which follows), and study the details and attributes of the proposed mascots.

Profile of John L. Lewis Elementary School

John L. Lewis Elementary School opened in 2005 in Floodrock, Illinois. Floodrock is located in Saline County in the very southern region of the state. The current enrollment at John L. Lewis is 315 students.

John L. Lewis Elementary is situated in an area that has two major businesses: farming and coal mining. The area has long been rich in coal mines, and many families in Saline County have had some connection to the coal mines. Since fewer homes and businesses depend on coal as an energy source these days, the activities in the mines have slowed, and the coal companies employ few residents. At the same time, the town of Floodrock and the rest of Saline County still associate themselves with the coal industry. That is why the citizens named the school after John L. Lewis, who was the president of the United Mine Workers of America for 40 years.

Figure 5–7. Proposed Mascots for John L. Lewis Elementary School

Manatee

Lowland Gorilla

Lemur

Miner

Ms. Alleman then leads a discussion in which the students identify and **EPISODE 2.5** assess the attributes associated with each potential mascot by answering these questions:

- What features or attributes do you associate with a *gorilla*?

- What features or attributes do you associate with a *miner*?

- What features or attributes do you associate with a *manatee*?

- What features or attributes do you associate with a *lemur*?

- How do these attributes match the criteria the class generated for selecting a good mascot?

Here is a bit of their discussion:

Nicholas: Manatees are kind of slow moving. You said yourself that some people call them sea cows. No one would want to think of himself as a sea cow.

Barbara: Gorillas are really strong. That would be good if you want to frighten the other teams. But gorillas have nothing to do with Illinois.

Nancy: And it doesn't sound right—the Lewis Gorillas.

Ms. Alleman: So what if it doesn't sound good?

Nancy: You want a mascot name that sounds right for the school. Then the cheers would sound right.

Ms. Alleman: How about the lemurs?

Ed: That sounds better—the Lewis Lemurs—but who would want to be a lemur? They are like shy little animals. The mascot has to be strong or powerful so that people want to be like it.

Ms. Alleman says that she expects each student to write a *thorough* and *logical* **EPISODE 2.6** paragraph about one of the proposed mascots and that she will demonstrate what a writer might think while composing one. She composes the following paragraph on a projected transparency, thinking out loud as she writes (her thoughts are shown in brackets):

The bobcat is a good example of a mascot for Gotha School. [*Why would I say that?*] A bobcat is a very smart animal and is a strong defender of its home and family. [*Why is this important?*] A student at Gotha can take pride in being represented by an animal that is a smart and strong protector of its family. [*But isn't a bobcat kind of scary?*] Although the bobcat can be an aggressive fighter, it attacks to survive and to protect its young, not to be mean.

The students then write their own paragraphs justifying their choice of a mascot for Lewis Elementary School (two typical examples are shown below).

> The miners are a good mascot for John L. Lewis elementary school. Everyone in the school can take pride in their past because their town was a mining town. Another thing miners have to be strong to get whatever they are mining. These characteristics are important because kids should be proud about their mascot, and their past.
>
> —Hannah, Grade 5

> The Lowland Gorilla is a good mascot for John L. Lewis school. A Lowland Gorilla is very intimidating, very smart, and is very strong and powerful. The Lowland Gorilla can make the students at John L. Lewis proud. All mascots should be strong and powerful so that the student can be proud and take pride in.
>
> —Kristian, Grade 5

Stage 3. Language Lesson: Learning Procedures for Using Coordinating Conjunctions

A written argument often uses coordinating conjunctions to qualify or expand on a statement. This is a good place in the instructional sequence to include a minilesson on how to use (and punctuate) coordinating conjunctions to clarify points in an argument (see Figure 5–8).

Stage 4. Applying the Procedures to a More Complex Problem

Students are now ready to consider more complicated problems using similar data sets but requiring more extensive analysis and explanation. Ms. Kelly's students at Thoreau School have recently enjoyed reading *Shiloh* and *Because of Winn-Dixie*, two novels that feature a dog that is important in the life of a family. Ms. Kelly decides this is a prime time for her students to explore finding appropriate homes for dogs available for adoption. Ms. Kelly's instruction includes small- and large-group discussions in which students negotiate how they are going to match dogs and prospective owners. Defending decisions that are questioned and challenged by their classmates, students engage in the same kind of thinking that will later guide their writing when they turn their notes into multiple-paragraph compositions.

Figure 5–8. Combining Sentences Using Coordinating Conjunctions

A coordinating conjunction is a word or small group of words that combines two parts of a sentence. Most commonly people use *and* for this purpose, as in the following sentences:

> Bob *and* Rhoda invested all of their money in a pyramid scheme.

> Now Bob is broke, *and* Rhoda is selling all of her jewelry on the Internet.

In the first of these two sentences, *and* is used to form a compound subject for the sentence, Bob *and* Rhoda. In the second sentence, *and* is used to form a compound sentence—that is, one in which there are two independent clauses connected by a coordinating conjunction (*and*). In other words, each of the two parts of the sentence can stand by itself, but they are combined into one by using *and*. Note how each of the following could stand alone as a complete sentence:

> Now Bob is broke.

> Rhoda is selling all of her jewelry on the Internet.

Using the coordinating conjunction *and*, we may combine these two sentences into this compound sentence: "Now Bob is broke, and Rhoda is selling all of her jewelry on the Internet."

In the exercise that follows, you are given two independent clauses (clauses that can stand alone as complete sentences). Use any of the following words to connect the two clauses into one:

hence	however
therefore	besides
moreover	consequently

When you use words from this list to connect two independent clauses, they should *follow a semicolon* and *be followed by a comma*, as in the following examples:

> I like Banana Slugs; *however*, they do benefit from a wee bit of salt.

> Manatees are soft and cuddly; *therefore*, I would rather have one as a pet than as a mascot.

> Wolverines can rip your flesh off; *moreover*, they can eat your vital organs.

(continues)

Figure 5–8. Combining Sentences Using Coordinating Conjunctions *(continued)*

For each of the following pairs of sentences, use a coordinating conjunction from the list to create a single compound sentence. Be sure to punctuate the sentences properly, using a semicolon before the conjunction and a comma following it.

1. The Lake Forest Academy Caxys is an excellent name.

   I think it wouldn't work for Lewis Elementary School.

2. I think that the name Wooden Shoes would be swell for a sports team.

   I don't see how you could play basketball in them.

3. Crystal Lake South High School north of Chicago calls its teams the Gators.

   They are 1,000 miles from the nearest alligator.

4. Webster University made up the name Gorloks for its teams.

   I suggest we call our teams the Lewis Laxtones.

5. I really love the taste of pretzels.

   I think that the name Pretzels would really rock for Lewis Elementary.

6. The Key School of Annapolis, Maryland, calls its teams the Ozebags.

   Few people know that it is an anagram for Gazebos.

7. I don't know how the St. Louis College of Pharmacy Eutectic picked its name.

   I don't think I want to know.

8. Presbyterian College calls its teams the Blue Hose.

   I would much rather wear White Sox.

9. I like the sound of the Chattanooga Central Purple Pounders.

   We should call our team the Lewis Mauve Marauders.

10. The Colby College teams are known as the White Mules.

    I find this name offensive to albinos.

Ms. Kelly introduces the problem by distributing a copy of a rescue center's pet adoption rules she created by looking at those found on the Internet (see Figure 5–9). To help students understand what rescue center workers do, Ms. Kelly has her students experience the process for themselves.

EPISODE 4.1

First, she has each student fill out a preadoption application form (sample forms are available on animal shelter websites).

Next Ms. Kelly displays a picture of a mature boxer: "Lady is a two-year-old boxer. She has lived in an apartment in the city with a young professional who had to leave the dog alone for long periods of time. Lady has not often been around people or other dogs, so she is rather shy. She loves to exercise, although she also enjoys periods of quiet companionship. Lady weighs 60 lbs."

Several students assess the dog's potential to fit in with their family, generating possibilities that they then modify in discussions with their classmates. One student offers: "She would fit right in. We already have two big dogs. We have a big fenced-in yard. Everyone at my house loves dogs. So

Figure 5–9. Pet Adoption Process

Background: Every day, Monday through Saturday, visitors come to the Floodrock Pet Rescue Center, in Floodrock, Illinois, in hopes of adopting a new pet. Of course, the workers at the rescue center care very much for the animals that they protect, and they want to place them in good homes, with loving and responsible pet owners. The workers cannot let people walk in and pick out any pet they want. The workers at the rescue center try to counsel potential owners about selecting the appropriate pet, so they have worked out a system.

Here is the process for dog adoption:

1. Each dog is categorized by its particular characteristics: big or small, companion or worker, leisurely or active, social or shy, etc. Each person who wants to adopt must fill out an application. The answers to the application questions help the rescue center workers know what kind of dog would be a good match for the person who wants to adopt it.

2. The rescue center manager reviews the dogs' profiles and the applications, meets with the people who want to adopt a pet, and recommends the best match. For example, a person who has a small apartment and spends most leisure time reading or watching television is not the best person to own a big dog that wants to exercise, run in open spaces, and meet other dogs and people.

she would be another member of the family." Other students suggest that she has overlooked some possible problems: two big dogs might already be enough for the family's available space, and the new dog might have trouble fitting in socially given her shyness.

Ms. Kelly divides the class into several smaller groups and gives them instructions for matching dogs with potential owners (Figure 5–10), along with a portfolio containing the necessary materials: six pictures and descriptions of dogs currently available for adoption, and profiles of four possible pet owners. After discussion, students individually prepare a written response.

Figure 5–10. Instructions for the Pet Adoption Activity

Your Job as a Team: This week there is a new group of visitors who want to adopt dogs, and there is a new bunch of dogs that are eligible for adoption.

1. Working with your partners, categorize the dogs ("couch potato," "busy bee," "free spirit," etc.), and then describe the characteristics of the best home and the most appropriate owner for each one of the dogs.

2. Study each application submitted by someone who wants to adopt a dog. Judge whether the person is suited to owning a dog and the best type of dog for that person. Discuss your decisions with your partners and explain why you have made the matches you did.

3. As you participate in the discussion, take notes about each person who has applied to adopt a dog. Write your notes in complete sentences. State the match and explain the reasons why the match is a good one. If someone is not an appropriate match for any dog, explain why.

4. In a whole-class discussion, explain the matches you recommend and why you recommend them. The class might have questions about your choices, so you'll want to be prepared to respond to those classmates who have doubts.

Writing About Your Matches: After you have discussed the possible matches thoroughly and have taken notes, write to Ms. Kay Neins, manager of Floodrock Pet Rescue Center, explaining the judgments you have made as you matched persons with pets. Ms. Neins is just returning from a long vacation and will have

(continues)

Figure 5–10. Instructions for the Pet Adoption Activity *(continued)*

to counsel the people who want to adopt a dog. Because she's been away, she is unfamiliar with the new dog arrivals and the new applicants. A letter from you will prepare her for her meetings with the hopeful owners. The following steps will guide you as you write your letter:

> *Step 1.* Using your notes, compose a draft letter to Ms. Kay Neins, manager of Floodrock Pet Rescue Center. You needn't bother with a personal introduction, but do let her know that you are aware of the challenge she faces in matching potential pet owners with the right dogs. The introduction will preview the discussion that follows. Also include a conclusion in which you review your judgments about matching persons with dogs. In short, your letter will have an introduction (noting the current problem), a paragraph about each potential dog owner and the appropriate dog, and a conclusion that generally reviews how to match people with dogs.
>
> *Step 2.* Allow other readers to examine the draft of your letter. You are probably proud of your work and will want to show it to family members and friends. In class, exchange your draft with a classmate. Allow your classmate to ask you questions for clarification. Your reviewers will probably check that you have applied the rescue center's guidelines for matching pets with owners, or they may want to know more about the dogs or the people interested in being dog owners. This is a clue that you need to explain or provide more details in your letter. Remember that Ms. Neins will not have all the pre-adoption applications and the dogs in front of her when she reads the letter. She will need *your* descriptions to help her recall the details. Also rely on your classmates and any available adult reader to help you with spelling, sentence and paragraph formation, and punctuation.
>
> *Step 3.* Rely on the questions and comments of your readers to guide you in rewriting your letter in a neat and corrected form. This should be a neat and error-free letter that can help Ms. Neins counsel the people who want to adopt a dog.

Olivia's letter is shown on the next page. Notice that Olivia states the problem and explains why it is significant. She recommends her matches systematically, citing the attributes of the dogs and the characteristics of the potential owner and the owner's environment. She also explains how she connected various details to arrive at her conclusions.

March 15

Dear Ms. Kay Neins,

I understand that you are struggling with pairing dogs with the right owners. For the sake of the pet and the owner, it is important to match the right dog with the most appropriate owner. I am writing to you to help you find homes for the dogs. I think some great pairs are the following: Emily Adamo and Bailey, Mike Lillis and Rascal, Mr. Smithers and Wolfie, and Vivian Glaussen and Shep.

I think that Bailey is a good dog for Emily Adamo. Bailey is a Golden Retriever. She is a good dog for Emily because Emily runs daily and Bailey is a running dog and can run with Emily every day. Emily works as a child psychologist and has three children of her own. She works in her home office from late in the afternoon into early evening hours. When she is at work she has a husband and three kids to watch over Bailey, who loves the company of humans. Bailey has a reputation for being good with children, so she will be a safe dog for Emily's children and for the young visitors to the home.

Rascal is probably a good dog for Mike Lillis because he lives and works on a farm, he wants a dog that can help him work on the farm and Rascal is a work dog. Rascal is a Dalmatian and dogs of that breed like to run. Mike works long hours and Rascal will be in the barn. There is no fence around Mike's yard but also there are not a lot of cars so he will not go running off into the streets. Rascal is a willing worker, but needs to be trained. Mike is an experienced farmer so he will be able to train him.

I think Wolfie is a good dog for Mr. Smithers. Wolfie is an Akita/Husky mix. He is a good dog for Mr. Smithers because he wants a guard dog and Wolfie is a guard dog. When Mr. Smithers is gone for nine hours, Wolfie will be able to stay home and be okay, because Wolfie is not very active because he is getting old. When Mr. Smithers is out for long hours, he will need a guard dog to watch over the house. Wolfie can do this job! While Mr. Smithers and his wife are not home, Wolfie will stay in the laundry room and the room is rather large so he will have room to walk and play around. In the winter when the Smithers are gone, the room is heated so Wolfie will stay warm. They have a fenced in yard with a chain linked fence about four feet high, so this gives him enough room to run around and play in a protected area. I think these two would be great companions.

I think a good dog for Vivian Glaussen is Shep, a mixed breed. It's a good dog for her because she is an older woman and does not need an active dog bouncing off the walls. She lives in a small condominium so he won't have that much place to run around. However, Vivian does not have a yard, so she will take Shep to a nearby park. She does not work out of her home, but while Ms. Glaussen volunteers and visits friends, Shep will be home alone for approximately twelve hours per week, or approximately two hours per day. Shep is cautious around children, but that is okay because Vivian does not have children.

Thank you for taking the time and reading my letter. I am glad that I had a chance to recommend how to pair these dogs with the right owners. I hope you approve of my choices because the suggestions should lead to strong long-term relationships between dogs and owners.

Respectfully,

Olivia

Olivia developed her response to this assignment through reasoned thought. Many elements in the process helped her do so:

1. Before small groups of students discussed the potential adoptions, they learned what the adoption process entailed.

2. Ms. Kelly had modeled the decision-making process.

3. Olivia benefited from small-group work with predetermined data. Disagreements within the groups forced students to explain why they had recommended their matches.

4. A structured note page prompted the students to record their decisions and the basis for them.

5. Before the students began writing, Ms. Kelly reminded them of their audience and the purpose of their letter. She also reviewed the evaluation criteria, outlining the specific traits that would distinguish a quality response.

6. As Olivia drafted her response, she shared it with classmates, who provided feedback about her reasoning and about the extent to which the composition matched the evaluation criteria.

7. Ms. Kelly conferred with Olivia and helped her edit the letter.

Extensions

1. Have students take the procedures they've learned and apply them to problems in other curricular areas in which analyzing data and persuading others is relevant. In science class they can argue for the

best diet for animals in the classroom terrarium, the conditions that result in water pollution, and so on. In history class they can argue the merits of different forms of government, the qualities of people running for elective office, and other aspects of civic participation. In language arts class they can argue which authors write the most interesting stories, which characters are responsible for which consequences, and so forth. In health class they can argue the consequences of diet, environmental exposure, and human or animal contact.

2. Have students conduct debates or mock trials on the issues they've written about.

3. Have students write letters to city administrators or local media or express and defend their opinions on a personal blog. By extending their argumentation beyond the classroom, students see that argumentation is not static but must respond to the particular expectations and conventions that govern appropriate and effective communication within different communities.

What Makes This Sequence a Structured Process Approach?

This instructional sequence helps younger students learn procedures for making claims, examining data that might support those claims, and warranting data as evidence for the claims. Older students can also be taught how to anticipate and rebut opposing positions. In any case, by working with their peers throughout the process, students undoubtedly hear objections to their perspectives; their final argument is therefore shaped in part by their awareness of potential counterarguments.

The activities progress from most accessible to more complex, providing a scaffold for grasping the principles of and procedures for argumentation. In the gateway activity students construct claims based on their own leisure pursuits, so they are able to formulate claims without having to also learn new information and concepts.

The second activity, considering and arguing in favor of an appropriate school mascot, takes the students out of their familiar world a bit but still allows them to apply their own beliefs. Also the task is open-ended; there is no single correct answer and various perspectives can flourish.

The instruction in how to use (and punctuate) coordinating conjunctions to clarify points in an argument is directly tied to the students' writing—it's designed to help students experiment with syntactic strategies for presenting sophisticated ideas in arguments as they coordinate a set of ideas in a single compound sentence.

The third activity, matching rescued dogs with new owners, takes students further outside their world of experience. Having to consider both new content and a new concept makes the task more abstract and therefore more complex.

The teachers featured in this chapter have worked outside class to plan activities that engage the students in class. In the first activity the preassembled materials prompt the students to produce their own data set. For the other two activities, teachers find strange or amusing school mascots on the Internet and prepare descriptions of dogs up for adoption and the people who might adopt them. Once the materials have been assembled and the activities conceived, the work is turned over to the students, who inductively develop procedures for making and substantiating claims. The teachers model *process* by thinking aloud while composing paragraphs in front of the class.

The students' work in class is highly social as they talk through the problems presented. Their discussions as they generate possible claims, relate them to the available evidence, and consider possible consequences are collaborative, critical, playful, experimental, and imaginative. Because the tasks are open-ended—though not to the point that any solution will do—there is room for students to make different yet equally plausible claims based on the same evidence, as is true in life.

Students learn how to think argumentatively and convert that thinking into written composition. The emphasis on procedures—learned inductively by participating in carefully sequenced activities that involve high levels of student activity and discussion related to the demands of a specific task—is a hallmark of a structured process approach to teaching.

Questions for Reflection

1. What associations do you think many students make when they hear the word *argument*? For the students, would the word generally have positive connotations, or negative ones? How would you know what students' impressions are?

2. If students generally have a sense that *argument* means something combative and competitive, how can you influence their thinking so that they are open to the use of argument in a constructive way?

3. Do you think of argument as a mode of writing? If it is a distinct mode of writing, how is it different from other modes? If *argument*

is a term that applies to a broad category of writing, how can such seemingly diverse types as definition, analysis, persuasion, and exposition be similar?

4. If you wanted students to develop skills in writing arguments over time, what sequence might you follow to introduce simple writing experiences and then progress systematically toward increasingly complex expressions?

5. How can frequent peer interaction in small groups and large groups play a key role in the development of skills in argument? How can you facilitate such interactions so that they are productive and not simply diversions?

6. To what extent is it reasonable to think of a standard model for argument? If argument is a relative cultural construct, how can learners adapt their thinking to account for multiple ways of making an argument?

7. What issues from the school or the community can serve as appropriate topics for discussion and for writing related arguments?

8. How can you construct learning activities that will engage students in the processes of argument and invite learners to reflect on those processes?

9. How will the study of argument support efforts to prepare students for state assessments of writing?

6

Teaching Comparison and Contrast Essays*

L ife presents many choices. Which candidate do we support for president? Which Wimbledon finalist do we root for? How do we get to work—in a car or on a bicycle? Where shall we dine out tonight—Nuevo Leon or El Sol?

Young people make choices all the time. They vote for candidates for school offices and homecoming courts. They choose classes to take, video games to play, social activities to pursue, a career path to investigate, a college to attend. These choices often involve comparing and contrasting the available options. Comparing and contrasting two or more possibilities is a central facet of living in a world that offers seemingly unlimited choices. It makes sense, then, to include comparison and contrast essays in the writing curriculum.

Comparison and contrast instruction often jumps in at the deep end: students' first assignment is to write an essay comparing Faulkner with Hemingway, Realism with Naturalism, Lear with Macbeth, Iraq with Vietnam, or other complex pairings. It makes sense to start with something more familiar and accessible so that students develop procedures before taking on topics that require more investigation and greater stretches in thinking.

---

*We would especially like to thank Angela Dean, for her contributions to this chapter.

The teaching sequence summarized in this chapter takes place in Angela Dean's classroom at Collins Hill High School, in Suwanee, Georgia. It is a suburban megaschool enrolling more than 3,700 students in the state's largest county, which borders Atlanta and reflects metro-area demographics.

Task Analysis

Angela's district relies heavily on accountability testing, which both changes teachers' priorities and creates impediments to teaching this sequence neatly. Late in the semester during which she taught this sequence, Angela wrote an email, updating us on her progress, and said:

> My environment this year has been much different from what I expected when I first agreed to teach the compare/contrast essay. We have mandated tests that I thought we'd take, blow off, and get down to the real stuff. This hasn't happened. I'm sorry to say that testing has frightened me into becoming a teacher of handouts and making sure I cover it all, because God only knows what they'll choose to put on the test. The extra testing days ate up time. We administer the PSAT; some of my kids take the Georgia high school graduation test and the county test, Gateway; we have our performance exams and then of course our unit tests and assessments. I've tried hard to complete the compare and contrast work alongside the curriculum, but there have been days that the curriculum has had to take center stage.

Sound familiar? Many if not most of us teach in districts like Angela's in which the need to demonstrate our accountability supersedes any commitment to teaching and learning. Satisfying these requirements is frustrating, but Angela's experience also offers a ray of hope: she did include the instruction, even if it took a lot longer than she anticipated. Any series of activities needs to be adapted to the instructional setting of teaching and learning, with some environments requiring more compromises than others.

The way we decide between two presidential candidates is a good starting point for helping students make similar kinds of choices. First, we need to *identify the points of comparison and contrast*—the issues on which we will compare and contrast the candidates. Figure 6–1 illustrates one possible way of placing the candidates' positions side by side. (Of course, a presidential race involves far more issues than those outlined, and more than two candidates.) With the points of comparison and contrast established, we then *characterize each candidate* relative to each point.

However, people may feel that one issue is more important than another or perhaps all others. For many people, the decision about the war overrides all the other considerations; their choice of candidate is thus clear and unambiguous. People concerned about global warming or immigration, areas in

Figure 6–1. Comparing and Contrasting Presidential Candidates

Issue	*Lauren Order*	*Conan Icecream*
Abortion	• Opposes abortion rights. • Has voted for abortion restrictions permissible under Roe v. Wade and would seek to overturn a guarantee of abortion rights. • Would not seek constitutional amendment to ban abortion.	• Favors abortion rights.
Death Penalty	• Supports expansion of the federal death penalty and limits on appeals.	• Supports death penalty for crimes for which the "community is justified in expressing the full measure of its outrage." • Supports videotaping interrogations and confessions in capital cases to minimize the possibility of wrongful convictions.
Education	• Favors parental choice of schools, such as vouchers for private schools and the right of parents to choose home schooling.	• Would encourage but not require universal prekindergarten programs, expand teacher mentoring programs, and reward teachers with higher pay not tied to standardized test scores. • Would change the national standardized testing program "so that we're not just teaching to a test and crowding out programs like art and music." • Favors a tax credit to pay up to $4,000 of college expenses for students who perform 100 hours of community service a year.
Global Warming	• Favors tougher fuel efficiency and laws that would cut greenhouse gas emissions by 60 percent by 2050. • Supports more nuclear power.	• Favors tougher fuel efficiency and laws that would cut greenhouse gas emissions by 60 percent by 2050. • Supports more nuclear power. • Proposes a 10-year, $150 billion program to produce climate-friendly energy supplies.

(continues)

Figure 6–1. Comparing and Contrasting Presidential Candidates *(continued)*

Issue	Lauren Order	Conan Icecream
Gun Control	• Opposes ban on assault-type weapons but favors requiring background checks at gun shows. • Would protect gun-makers and dealers from civil suits. • Opposes gun control.	• Believes gun-makers and dealers should be open to lawsuits. • Supports a ban on all forms of semiautomatic weapons and tighter restrictions on firearms.
Health Care	• Opposes universal coverage. • Proposes a $2,500 refundable tax credit for individuals and $5,000 for families to make health insurance more affordable.	• Seeks universal coverage by requiring employers to share costs of insuring workers. • Would raise taxes on wealthiest families to finance the program.
Immigration	• Supports border fence. • Wants to allow illegal immigrants to stay in the U.S., work, and apply to become legal residents after they learn English, pay fines and back taxes, and clear a background check.	• Supports border fence. • Wants to offer legal status to illegal immigrants subject to conditions, including learning English and paying back taxes and fines.
The War	• Opposes scheduling a troop withdrawal because she believes "the surge" is working. • Supported the original invasion but criticized the manner in which the administration went about it. • Supports troop increases and the construction of bases for permanent U.S. occupancy.	• Opposed war at start, opposed troop increase later. • Proposes to withdraw all combat troops by end of the decade.

which the candidates appear to have rather similar policies, will need to pay greater attention to other issues. In order to make a good decision, then, voters need to *create priorities* about which issues matter most and rank them from most to least important. Doing so often requires *making a value judgment,* such as "Lauren Order's position on gun control allows for an armed citizenry, which will deter crime," or "Conan Icecream's position on gun control will reduce the overall availability of guns, which will deter crime." With either position viable, voters need to make an evidence-based choice.

Here is a set of procedures people might use to compare and contrast two potential choices:

- Identify the points of comparison and contrast.

- Characterize each choice in terms of the points of comparison and contrast.

- Create priorities among the points of comparison and contrast.

- Compare and contrast the two choices.

- Make a value judgment.

These procedures might or might not be linear. For instance, creating priorities might come first: a voter might see candidates' positions on abortion to be so important at the outset that everything else falls into line behind it. Then again, the process of comparing and contrasting might elevate the importance of other issues and even change one's initial value judgments.

Next we need to design a set of comparison and contrast activities that will enable students to write essays explaining the value of each option. Planning such instruction involves several considerations. One decision concerns the topics to be compared and contrasted. Ultimately, students will select their own topics. But for whole-class instruction in the procedures, areas of common interest seem appropriate. Asking students for topics related to their own social world is a good way to start.

Stage 1. Gateway Activity: Analyzing Similarities and Differences

Angela announces, "Today we're going to begin working on comparison and contrast essays. We'll start by talking about two things that are relatively similar. So how about recommending two things of the same type for our discussion: two fast-food restaurants, two musicians who perform the same genre, two athletes who play the same position, two celebrities who are in the headlines, or any other pair of similar people, places, or things you would like to compare and contrast. But please, nothing that will make me blush, and don't pick two people from our school."

Angela's students decide to compare and contrast two radio stations that many of the students listen to: how are the two radio stations similar and different? Angela records their contributions on the board, creating a column for each station. The students point out that while both stations play a core of mainstream rock, they are different in a number of ways: one plays more

EPISODE 1.1

urban and hip-hop music, while the other plays more country and western; one has more political features, while the other's disc jockeys talk more about celebrities; one pairs men with women for their drive-time broadcasts, while the other's disc jockeys behave like frat boys; one has interviews with musicians while the other has an afternoon sports show.

After recording the comments, Angela asks students to categorize the points they have made. The students note that their observations could be classified according to the genres of music played, the kinds of disc jockeys employed, and the nonmusical features of the programming. Angela then creates a chart similar to the graphic used for comparing political candidates in Figure 6–1. She lists the categories for comparison and contrast in the left column and the examples for the two radio stations in the next two columns. She explains that they have *identified the points of comparison and contrast* between the two stations and *characterized each station* according to the points of comparison and contrast.

She then asks the students if they consider any of these categories more important than the others. One student says that the type of music is paramount; another feels the quality of the banter between disc jockeys rules; still another insists the celebrity features trump all. Angela identifies this additional feature of comparing and contrasting: *creating priorities among the points of comparison and contrast* in order to refine the task and personalize the process.

EPISODE 1.2   In small groups the students:

- Compare and contrast the two stations in relation to each point of comparison and contrast.

- Make a value judgment about which of the two stations they prefer.

When they finish, they report back to their classmates, who have the opportunity to raise questions about each group's thinking. Students are therefore prompted to think critically about their decisions and are responsible for communicating their ideas and reactions, areas in which teachers usually tend to dominate classrooms (see Marshall et al. 1995 and Nystrand 1997). This shift puts students in greater control of their own learning.

Thus far in this instruction, students have done a lot more talking than writing. Talking about the issues becomes the basis for their later writing: the students experience the processes they will employ and get feedback on their thinking in real time. The writing will potentially yield new insights, but discussion at this early stage is a powerful way for students to learn thinking processes they can later apply to similar tasks.

Stage 2. Applying Comparison and Contrast Procedures to a New Task

Moving toward independence, students compare and contrast elements they have chosen themselves—and which they will not need to research— thus increasing their ability to be successful. Students might compare a Ford pickup with a Chevrolet pickup, the soccer player Ronaldo with his fellow Brazilian Ronaldinho, one line of cosmetics with another, the *Dragon Ball* manga series to the *Dragonquest* manga series, one baba ghanoush recipe with another, Sunnis with Shiites, Cantonese eggrolls with Philippine eggrolls, Oprah with Ellen—the possibilities are endless.

Angela begins by saying, "Next, in small groups, select two places, people, or things, or events to compare and contrast. Pick things you know a lot about so you'll be well informed about them. You may pick any school-appropriate pair of items that are more or less similar: two pizza parlors, two musicians in the same genre, two cars from the same class, two stores of the same type, and so on. But remember, nothing that will make me blush or require me to call your parents. And don't use two people from our school." As a reminder she projects a list of the steps in the process:

EPISODE 2.1

- Identify the points of comparison and contrast between the two items.

- Characterize each item in relation to the points of comparison and contrast.

- Create priorities among the points of comparison and contrast.

- Compare and contrast the two items.

- Make a value judgment.

She also stresses that this list is not a strict sequence; they just need to be sure to include each of these procedures somewhere along the way. She tells them they have thirty minutes. (If there is time and the technology is available, students can supplement their own knowledge with information from the Internet or other sources.)

Three boys who are taking technical preparatory classes decide to compare two basketball players, Kobe Bryant and Tracy McGrady, both of whom went straight from high school to professional basketball, are roughly the same height, and play the same position. Angela asks them to develop three or four categories of comparison and contrast for their essay and make a value judgment. The students settle on the categories of physical features,

Figure 6–2. Points of Comparison/Contrast: Kobe Bryant vs. Tracy McGrady

Kobe Bryant	Tracy McGrady
African American	African American
MVP 2008	Houston Rockets
Los Angeles Lakers	Adidas
Nike Lowtops	Rookie of the year
Hops, jumps over car	Captain
Fade-away	15 pts per game
Captain	6'8"
6'7"	Straight from N.C. private high school
27.1 pts per game	11 yrs pro
Ball hog/fast	223 lbs
Straight from Lower Merion HS	30 yrs old
12 yrs pro	Won community award
205 lbs	Player in Olympics
National high school Player of the year	
Youngest player in NBA	
Player in Olympics	

statistics, and accomplishments, and conclude that Kobe Bryant is a better player than Tracy McGrady. The points of comparison they identify are listed in Figure 6–2.

EPISODE 2.2   After completing their comparison and contrast, each group reports back to the class; some students use presentation software. Their classmates question and critique their work, and the groups either defend or revise their conclusion. Reflecting on their process and sharing these reflections makes students consciously aware of the procedures they are learning.

Stage 3. Generating Task-Specific Evaluative Criteria

One way to help students develop evaluative standards is to ask them to consider the qualities of a set of comparison and contrast essays and generate their own criteria based on their assessment.

EPISODE 3.1   Angela presents the assignment:

> You will read three essays comparing and contrasting two breakfast cereals. Your task is to work in a small group with classmates to decide which essay is best, which is second best, and which is third best. Each small group will represent one of the following types of readers:

- Readers evaluating the state writing test.

- High school English teachers.

- Hungry teenagers who can't decide what to eat for breakfast.

- Representatives from the manufacturers of the cereal companies.

- Parents who must be convinced which cereal to buy for their teenagers.

- Lumberjacks who are unfamiliar with the brands and can only buy one box of cereal before a big day of chopping down trees.

As you work, take notes, because you will need to explain the reasons behind your ranking.

The three essays (A, B, and C) are shown here. Each deliberately has some positive qualities and some problems. Students also have to tease out whether the readers *they* represent would value organization over insight, correct standard English over a strong voice, and so on.

Essay A

In this essay I will compare two cereals that are very similar, Oat Loops and Früt Boops. Both have many similarities. Each one is a breakfast cereal. Each one is shaped like a little tire. Each one is yummy. But in fact, they are also very different. I will next explain why.

Oat Loops is made by the Giant Foods Corporation in the USA, which is ironic because each Oat Loop is in fact quite small. Früt Boops is made by the Kloggs company, which is also ironic because it is a high fiber cereal. So that's one difference right there, even though they are also similar.

Both Oat Loops and Früt Boops have ingredients. But the ingredients are different. In Oat Loops you will find whole grain oats, modified corn starch, corn starch, sugar, salt, trisodium phosphate, calcium carbonate, mono-glycerides, tocopherols, wheat starch, and annatto. On the other hand, in Früt Boops there is sugar, corn flour, wheat flour, oat flour, partially hydro-genated vegetable oil (one or more of: coconut, cottonseed, and soybean), salt, sodium ascorbate, ascorbic acid, natural orange, lemon, cherry, rasp-berry, blueberry, lime, other natural flavors, red #40, blue #2, yellow #6, zinc oxide, niacinamide, turmeric color, blue #1, annatto color bht (preser-vative), and folic acid. As you can see, the ingredients are different, and Früt Boops has many more ingredients.

There are other differences too. In Oat Loops you will find the daily mini-mum requirement of many important vitamins. You get 0% for vitamin A, 0% for vitamin C, 4% for calcium, 35% for iron, 0% for vitamin D, 5% for thiamine, 3% for riboflavin, 5% for niacin, 15% for vitamin B-6, 10% for folate, 0% for vitamin B-12, 5% for pantothenate, 7% for phosphorus, 10% for magnesium, and 10% for zinc. You get even more of these things if you add milk. On the other hand, in Früt Boops you will find 4% for vitamin A, 7% for vitamin C, 0% for calcium, 15% for iron, 10% for vitamin D, 4% for thiamine, 0% for riboflavin, 9% for niacin, 11% for vitamin B-6, 12% for folate, 0% for vitamin B-12, 15% for pantothenate, 6% for phosphorus, 9% for magnesium, and 18% for zinc. As is the case with Oat Loops, you get more of each one if you add milk. The only way in which they are the same is that both provide 0% of your daily vitamin B-12 needs, although that probably changes if you add milk.

In conclusion, Oat Loops and Früt Boops are both cereals that you can eat for breakfast or other meals, or snacks. Both are delicious. I recommend that you eat Früt Boops because with fruit it is healthier and the additional ingredients make it even healthier. And if you add milk, you will have a nutritious, delicious breakfast.

Essay B

Oat Loops and Früt Boops are both breakfast cereals they are similar and different in many ways. I will next tell you how. The flavor of the two is really different, Oat Loops as the name suggests is made mainly from oats and so has an oati flavor. Its also lite on sugar and so you taste oats more than sweetness. Whereas Früt Boops first ingredient is sugar not flour and so its way sweet which many people like. Both are shaped exactly the same like a little bagel and they are equally crunchy as long as you dont add too much milk. Both are deciduous. Oat Loops are also healthier because its pretty much just oats in their and there healthy. Whereas Früt Boops needs color so it has got alot of fake colors like red #40, blue #2, yellow #6, turmeric color, blue #1, & annatto color bht whatever that is. Both cereals come in many varieties Oat Loops comes in Honey Heaven, Berry Bunches, Yogurt Yummys, Multigrain Crunchios, Fruitios Frostios, and Apple Raisin. Whereas Früt Boops comes in Marshmallow Boops, Low Sugar Boops, Big Bang Boops with caffeine, and Früt Boops–flavored Toast-R Tarts. These choices give you plenty of variety expecially when you buy the variety pack. In conclusion I recommend that you eat Oat Loops instead of Früt Boops because they are healthier because they're first ingredient is oats not sugar and because they do not have fake colors to stimulate fruit colors. Just add milk and youll have an even healthier way to start your day.

Essay C

Many people begin their day with a nice bowl of cereal. Often they have to start the day by choosing between two kinds. Suppose you got up one day and were hungry and opened the cabinet and found one box of Oat Loops and one box of Früt Boops and had to make a choice. What would you do? I often solve problems like this by writing an essay comparing and contrasting the two things. So that is what I will do now. By the end of my essay I will convince you that the best way to start your day is with a delicious bowl of Früt Boops.

Both of these cereals are delicious and nutritious and are shaped like little donuts. Just reading the side of the box makes me want to get out a bowl and a spoon and some milk and dig in. For example Oat Loops is full of delicious oats which may lower cholesterol which is why it is certified by the American Heart Association. It also contains 14 vitamins & minerals, is low in fat, has less then 3 grams of fat in each serving, has 10% of the calcium you need for the day, has plenty of fiber, has only 1 gram of sugar, is a good source of iron, and may reduce the risk of heart disease as part of a heart-healthy diet. Früt Boops are also delicious but not because of oats, because of the sweet and fruity flavor. The very first ingredient in Früt Boops is sugar which means that there's more sugar in it than anything else. Mmmmmmmm. Furthermore Früt Boops ingredients include many extra flavors including orange, lemon, cherry, raspberry, blueberry, lime, and other natural flavors. Because they are natural they are healthy and so good for you. Früt Boops also includes oats which are in Oat Loops and also corn and wheat, which gives them the triple whammy of nutrition. And the corn that they use contains traces of soybeans, which are especially healthy. As you can see both of these cereals are delicious and healthy because of their many totally excellent ingredients. So how do you choose between them.

I believe that Früt Boops provide the best breakfast to start the day because they have so many healthy ingredients and a nice sweet taste that gets rid of "morning breath" too. And the healthy amount of sugar gives you that extra energy you need to get you going in the morning, especially if you get Big Bang Boops with Caffeine. And so in conclusion, my comparison and contrast of Oat Loops and Früt Boops proves that for a healthy, deliciously sweet breakfast that gets you going without morning breath, Früt Boops is the way to start your day.

Angela asks the groups to choose which audience they want to represent. After each group selects the audience it will role-play, the whole class then discusses what they think each particular group will look for in each essay.

Here's what they say:

1. State evaluators will look first to mechanical aspects of the essay and whether spelling or grammar mistakes stand out; accuracy in details provided is also a consideration. These readers will look for a logical argument in which the writer stays on topic and maintains an organized presentation of ideas. Since teachers will most likely have the same concerns, one of the small groups will represent both viewpoints.

2. Teens will be more concerned with descriptions of the cereals; they want to be able to imagine what the cereal looks like and how it tastes.

3. First and foremost, manufacturers want to know what aspects of the cereal they can use as selling points and how best to market their product; taste is important, as well as any other information they can use to create advertisements, persuade the consumers, and bring in profits.

4. Parents will place nutrition and price first; they'll want to know how it might help or hurt their child nutritionally. Brand is also important. If they know and trust the brand, parents will purchase the cereal for their children.

5. The amount of servings per box will be important to the lumberjacks, along with nutrition and how filling the cereal is. Price is also significant, since lumberjacks work hard and don't want to waste money on unhealthy food. Lumberjacks want a cereal that helps them feel energized and ready for a long day at work.

The members of the state evaluator/teacher group choose Essay C as the strongest because it has a clear thesis, the opening and closing paragraphs are strong, it supports its argument with details, and it is more mechanically sound than the other essays. They also feel the essay isn't overly opinionated and flows well. They rate Essay A next: it emphasizes comparing and contrasting equally and is persuasive. However the mechanical aspects are not as strong as Essay C's. They place Essay B last. Its opinions and facts are not as thorough, and it doesn't seem to be aimed at an audience of this kind.

The teen group and the manufacturing group both place the essays in the same order. Essay B emphasizes taste over factual information, and how the cereals taste is of greatest importance to the consumers (the teens) and the manufacturers (as a selling point). They rank Essay C next. The opinions and the description of the cereal it offers are important to both groups. Although the essay doesn't mention nutrition, probably neither group is concerned with the product's nutritional value. They place Essay A last because it focuses solely on facts and nutrition and therefore doesn't speak to these groups.

The parent group ranks the essays in letter order: A, B, and C. Essay A addresses parents' concern for ingredients; Essay B speaks to the nutritional value parents may worry about; and Essay C only deals with taste, which is not a significant concern for this audience.

The lumberjacks group is most drawn to Essay C, because their number one concern is how filling a cereal might be, given the kind of work they do. They rank Essay A second because it speaks to nutrition—lumberjacks don't want to put something of no nutritional value in their bodies. They place Essay B last because it doesn't address how filling and nutritious the cereals are.

The students generate *criteria* they believe should be applied to writing of this sort. Differences in the readerships represented by the different groups are acknowledged, and the extent to which writing quality has universal criteria or depends on the expectations of anticipated readers is considered.

EPISODE 3.2

Students, in small groups, use a template (available on web sources such as www.rubistar.com or www.learner.org/workshops/hswriting/interactives/rubric) to construct the *rubric* by which their comparison and contrast essays will be evaluated. Students inevitably reconsider their original criteria in light of their exchanges with other groups. Ideally, this process helps students overcome whatever bias exists in their original assumptions and move their thinking to a new and broader consideration of what is involved in a comparison and contrast of two items of a similar type, presented to a particular community of readers.

EPISODE 3.3

Each group reports to the class, displaying their rubric through an overhead projector or by some other means. Students from other groups offer critiques that prompt additional discussion of the assessment criteria, and Angela helps the class settle on a single rubric for grading the essays.

EPISODE 3.4

The group rubrics range from four criteria to eight criteria. Angela asks them to consider how a student might feel receiving a rubric with many criteria or one with only four or five criteria. She shows them a rubric with fifteen criteria, which they find quite overwhelming. Many say that if they were given such a long list, they wouldn't bother to write—they'd feel they could never meet the standards and get a good grade. They begin discussing which criteria they feel must stay and which can go.

Angela reiterates the requirements of a compare and contrast essay: identifying two things that have similarities and differences, collecting details regarding each item, organizing the details into categories, ranking these categories in order of importance, and finally creating a value judgment. She wants them to see how these steps lead to the requirements of a compare and contrast essay. The value judgment is linked to a strong thesis statement. The details provide support for the argument. Creating and ranking categories prompts the essay's organization and paragraph development.

Next, the class discusses evaluative rankings: numbers (four to one or one to four), usually linked to descriptors such as *advanced, proficient, basic,* or *needs improvement.* Angela writes a list of descriptors on the board, and the class whittles away at it, making their own unique list. Students discuss the pros and cons of each descriptor and how they might feel as writers if their work were categorized that way.

Many jump on the descriptors *needs improvement, weak,* and *unacceptable,* saying these terms make them feel they have nothing to offer. They are adamant that if they received a label like this on a writing assignment, they wouldn't want to write any longer. They have hit on the important idea that we must look for what is present in the writing rather than focusing on what the writing lacks, thus nurturing reluctant writers rather than making them question their decision to take risks and make an effort. The class settles on the following descriptors: *advanced, accomplished, improving,* and *emerging.*

The class then discusses what the rubric should evaluate. Students feel that organization should be the first requirement, because the essay needs to flow logically so that the reader can easily follow the writer's argument and supporting details. They decide to combine the criteria for organization and paragraph development into a single area. Details become the next criterion: accurate information is necessary to support the overall argument and persuade the reader to see things from the writer's perspective.

The students also combine audience and tone into one area, since one cannot consider audience without thinking about the tone of the piece. An audience isn't likely to respond to an argument presented in a supercilious or argumentative tone. The class puts grammar, spelling, and punctuation as the last criteria. (The final rubric is shown in Figure 6–3.)

At the end of the session, Angela says, "Look back to our rubric. Is there anything your group might change, considering your audience? If so, make the changes or additions and provide a reason for your changes."

The group writing about Kobe Bryant and Tracy McGrady makes the following elaborations:

Kobe is a better player than Tracy.

    I.   Kobe has better statistics.
          A.   For example, Kobe averages 27.1 points per game; McGrady averages 15 points per game.

Figure 6–3. A Rubric for Evaluating Comparison and Contrast Essays

	Advanced (4)	Accomplished (3)	Improving (2)	Emerging (1)
Organization and Paragraph Development	Logical presentation of ideas; all parts contribute to a strong central idea; each paragraph always relates to the topic and presents details that allow the reader to understand the argument more completely; paragraphs flow seamlessly from one to the other.	Most ideas are connected; some parts contribute to the central idea; many paragraphs relate to the topic and often present convincing details; paragraphs flow seamlessly from one to the other.	Some ideas connected to each other; many parts don't contribute to the central idea; some paragraphs relate to the topic and present convincing details that support the argument; transitions between paragraphs are sometimes smooth.	Ideas have little connection to each other; there is no strong central idea; few or no paragraphs relate to the topic; transitions between paragraphs are awkward.
Details	Uses details that are always accurate, appropriate, and that fully support the topic.	Uses details that are mostly accurate and typically support the topic.	Uses some details that are accurate; some details are not appropriate for the topic; details do not always support the topic.	Uses little or no detail to support and explain the topic.
Audience and Tone	The writer has correctly identified the intended audience; writing shows a complete understanding of audience's expectations; tone matches the intent of the piece appropriately, enhancing the reader's experience and understanding.	The writer has correctly identified the intended audience; writing shows that the writer is somewhat aware of the audience's expectations; appropriate tone is consistently maintained throughout the piece.	The writer has an incomplete idea of the audience and its expectations; inconsistent tone, or tone consistent in some parts but not the entire essay.	The writer has not identified the audience; writing does not address a specific audience; tone is not appropriate for the topic or audience.
Grammar, Punctuation, Spelling	Uses completely appropriate grammar that helps readers understand meaning; no errors in punctuation; all words are spelled correctly, helping readers clearly understand the central idea.	Uses appropriate grammar that does not interfere with meaning; a few punctuation errors; most words are spelled correctly.	Grammar choices sometimes confuse readers; many or major errors in punctuation that sometimes confuse the reader; many spelling errors sometimes make it hard for the reader to understand the central idea.	Grammar choices keep readers from understanding the piece; frequent and/or major errors in spelling that obscure meaning; frequent spelling errors make it hard for the reader to understand the central idea.

> ~~B.~~ ~~Kobe and McGrady can both shoot 3s, but Kobe has a sick~~
> fade-away.
>
> C. Kobe has 12 yrs in the NBA; McGrady has 11 yrs in the
> NBA.

II. Kobe has more accomplishments than McGrady.
   A. Kobe has been awarded the MVP, in 2008; McGrady hasn't.
   B. They both played in 2008 Olympics.
   C. They were both Rookie of the Year.

Their final outline is shown here.

Kobe Bryant vs. Tracy McGrady Comparison/Contrast Essay

TS: Topic Sentence
D: Data
W: Warrant
CS: Concluding Statement

Introduction: In the NBA, there are many great teams. Over all there are two teams with incredible players. The Rockets and the Lakers. These two athletes are Kobe Bryant and Tracy McGrady. They have many skills that we will talk about.

Thesis: Kobe is a better player than Tracy.

Body Paragraph 1

(TS): Kobe is a better player statistically.

(D): Kobe averages 27.1 points per game; McGrady averages 15 points per game.

(W): This shows that Kobe is better on the court at shooting and makes up most of his team's points.

(W): This shows that Kobe is a bit of a ball-hog, but it's for the good of the team.

(D): Kobe and McGrady can both shoot 3s; but Kobe has a sick fade-away.

(W): They can both shoot 3s pretty good, but when they are blocked, Kobe can resort to his fade-away.

(W): Kobe is better, because he has more than one method to score and get more points. Plus, Kobe has a better style of shooting.

(D): Kobe has 12 yrs in the NBA; McGrady has 11 yrs in the NBA.

(W): They both have been around for a while, but Kobe has a bit more experience than T-Mac, which makes him better.

(W): But as we can tell, they are both seasoned veterans.

(CS): In conclusion, Kobe is a better player because he has more years, better shooting, more points than McGrady.

Body Paragraph 2

(TS): Kobe has more accomplishments than McGrady.

(D): Kobe has been awarded MVP, in 2008; McGrady hasn't.

(W): This shows that Kobe has been successful in 2008 and he got awarded for playing good.

(W): This shows that McGrady is playing good, but not as good as Kobe.

(D): They both played in 2008 Olympics.

(W): This shows that they both played really good in the '08 season and went to the Olympics.

(W): This shows that they have enough skill to impress the U.S. coach and earn a spot on the national team.

(D): Kobe also got high school player of the year and McGrady didn't.

(D): They were both Rookie of the Year.

(W): This shows that they were talented coming into the pros and playing their best in their rookie year.

(CS): In conclusion, Kobe is a better athlete than T-Mac because he has earned more awards than McGrady.

Conclusion: In conclusion, to our information, you can clearly see that Kobe Bryant is a better player than Tracy McGrady. Stats show that advantage Kobe has over Tracy.

Stage 4. Writing in Small Groups

Students now attempt their first writing, in the same small groups that generated the information. Composing as a group, students learn how to put information into an appropriate form in a situation in which they can co-construct knowledge and receive continual feedback on their thinking (see Dale 1997).

EPISODE 4.1 Each group specifies the community of readers who will evaluate their essay, revising the class rubric as necessary. Here's the assignment:

> In your small group, compose an essay in which you compare and contrast two school-appropriate people, places, things, or events of your choice. Remember the procedures we have used in our discussions thus far:
>
> 1. Make sure you compare and contrast two items that are generally similar yet different in ways you can identify and explain.
>
> 2. Before you begin writing:
>
>   a. Identify the points of comparison and contrast between the two items.
>
>   b. Characterize each item in relation to the points of comparison and contrast.
>
>   c. Create priorities among the points of comparison and contrast.
>
>   d. Compare and contrast the two items.
>
>   e. Make a value judgment about the two items.
>
> 3. Using the rubric you have prepared as your guide, compose an essay in which you present and support your comparison and contrast.

Angela circulates among the groups as they work, keeping the students on task and answering their questions. The group comparing Bryant and McGrady, writing for an audience of coaches, staff members, fans, youth, and teachers, produces the essay shown here.

Group Essay on Kobe Bryant vs. Tracy McGrady

In the NBA, there are many great teams. Over all, there are two teams with incredible players. The Rockets and the Lakers. These two athletes are Kobe Bryant and Tracy McGrady. They have many skills that we will talk about.

Kobe is a better player statistically. He averages 27.1 points per game, while McGrady averages 15 points per game. This shows that Kobe is better on the court at shooting and makes up most of this team's points. This also shows that Kobe is a bit of a ball-hog, but it's good for the team. Another detail is that both Kobe and McGrady can shoot 3s, but Kobe has a sick fade-away. This shows that Kobe can resort to his fade-away if he's blocked, but McGrady can't. This also shows that Kobe is better because he has more than one method to score. Kobe also has a better style of shooting. The last detail is that Kobe has 12 yrs in the NBA, while McGrady has 11 yrs in the NBA. This proves that Kobe is better because Kobe has more experience playing. Still, you can tell they are both seasoned veterans. In conclusion, Kobe is better statistically because he has more years playing, he has better shooting, and he averages more points than McGrady.

Kobe has more accomplishments than McGrady. Kobe has been awarded MVP, in 2008, and McGrady hasn't. This shows that Kobe has worked hard during the season and was awarded at the end. This also shows that McGrady has been playing good, but not as good as Kobe. Kobe played in the 2008 Olympics. This shows that Kobe is better because he played to his potential and was able to impress the coach of the United States team. They were both Rookie of the Year. This shows that they were talented coming into the pros and playing their best in their first year. Kobe also got a high school player of the year award and McGrady didn't. In conclusion, Kobe is a better athlete than T-Mac because he has earned more awards than McGrady.

In conclusion, to our information, you can clearly see that Kobe Bryant is a better player than Tracy McGrady. Stats show that advantage Kobe has over Tracy. Accomplishments, awards, and their number of years in the NBA also show that Kobe is better.

When a group completes its essay, the members present a written copy to a different group, who role-play being members of the intended audience and use the class rubric to evaluate the essay and submit an assessment. Each peer response group discusses the essay and assigns the essay a letter grade based on the rubric's rankings and provides a written explanation of how the writers performed in relation to each assessment criteria.   **EPISODE 4.2**

The small groups revise their essays and receive a grade from Angela, who uses the rubrics developed by the class. The students also write informal reflections on how they went about writing their essays. This attention to their writing process enables students to name the processes they have developed so they may consciously apply them in the future.   **EPISODE 4.3**

Figure 6–4. Combining Sentences Using Subordinating Conjunctions

A subordinating conjunction connects two types of clauses:

- An independent clause (one that can stand on its own as a complete sentence).

- A dependent clause (one that cannot stand on its own and must be attached to an independent clause).

Common subordinating conjunctions include the following words:

after	if	till
although	once	until
as	since	when
because	than	where
before	that	whether
how	though	while

Here are some examples of these words acting as subordinating conjunctions. Note that either the independent or the dependent clause may come first in the sentence.

> *Until* someone convinces me otherwise, I'll take Oat Loops over Früt Boops any day.

> I prefer Früt Boops over Oat Loops, *though* some days their sugary sweetness makes my teeth ache.
> *After* I eat dinner, I often eat a giant bowl of Oat Loops for dessert.

> Früt Boops–flavored Toast-R Tarts are delicious *because* they have so much extra sugar in them.

In the exercise that follows, you are provided with two clauses. Connect them using one of the subordinating conjunctions from the list in order to form a complex sentence.

1. Some people prefer listening to the tenor saxophone.

   I would rather hear the soprano.

2. El Toro serves its chips hot and crisp.

   At Los Compadres the chips are served cold and soggy.

(continues)

Figure 6–4. Combining Sentences Using Subordinating Conjunctions *(continued)*

3. The Times New Roman font is a big favorite.

   I like Ariel much better.

4. The Jack Russell Terrier is a very popular breed of dog.

   I find them to be rather nippy, yippy, and zippy.

5. Olson's Hardware Store carries many types of hex nuts.

   Generic Tools only has the standard sizes.

6. The red buckeye flowers early in the spring.

   White buckeyes flower in mid-summer.

7. Bill Cosby talks a lot about his family in his comedy.

   Eddie Izzard talks more about history.

8. Truck commercials seem targeted to tough guys.

   Minivan commercials are designed for family consumers.

9. Chinese egg rolls are filling and come in a wheat dough wrapper.

   Vietnamese egg rolls are wrapped in rice paper and are lighter.

10. In Season One of *24*, Jack Bauer was married to Teri.

    In Season Two Jack's girlfriend was Kate Warner.

Stage 5. Language Lesson: Using Subordinating Conjunctions

Comparing and contrasting two things often involves using sentences that include subordinating conjunctions—words such as *although* and *since* that qualify a statement. The exercise in Figure 6–4 helps students construct complex sentences (those including both an independent and a dependent clause) by using subordinating conjunctions.

Stage 6. Writing from Sources

Thus far students have been dealing with familiar topics and have been able to rely on their personal knowledge to provide the content for their essays. Now they begin working with less familiar, more complex topics that require consulting sources for information.

Nelson and Hayes (1988), investigating how college students approached writing from sources, found that weaker students went on fact-finding missions and then reproduced their sources' ideas verbatim. Stronger students found information that helped them argue a position and looked at the source material from an original perspective. Writers should not simply juxtapose pieces of information; they should use the information to draw an original and forceful conclusion.

In the following activity students use a relatively small set of sources in order to compare and contrast two singing groups with whom they are likely unfamiliar. Rather than just saying that the groups are similar and different in various ways, the students choose one singing group over another based on their comparison and contrast.

EPISODE 6.1   Angela gives her students the following task:

> You and a group of friends are attending a small musical festival with two sound stages. The second set features two groups with which you are not familiar: the Bobs and the Persuasions. (These are real groups.) Each group sings *a cappella*—that is, without musical accompaniment. While similar in many ways, there are key differences between the two. You need to choose which of the two performances you will attend. Fortunately, the music program you bought as a souvenir includes descriptions of both bands.

"Who Are the Bobs?" and "Who Are the Persuasions?" describe the two singing groups. Angela tells the students they may also use the Internet features of their phones to get additional information to help them make their decision. As they work, she circulates among the groups, monitoring their work and answering their questions.

Who Are the Bobs?

The Bobs
Official website: www.bobs.com

The Bobs are a "new wave" a cappella group that originally came from San Francisco. At the time of their formation, the members of the band delivered singing telegrams, but when Western Union folded in 1981, they became unemployed. Gunnar Madsen and Matthew Stull were among these now-out-of-work singers. They loved singing together and wanted to form an a cappella singing group so they could continue singing for a living. They placed a small classified advertisement looking for a bass singer and got one call, from Richard "Bob" Greene, who not only sang bass but also wrote songs and had experience as a recording engineer.

Their first show was at an open mike in a Cuban restaurant where they sang "Psycho Killer" by the Talking Heads, "Helter Skelter" by the Beatles, and other songs rarely sung by a cappella groups. The audience found them different and amusing and responded enthusiastically. In their other early shows they sang other popular songs with new and innovative arrangements, but soon they began writing their own material, also with unusual arrangements. These new songs often required an additional voice. As they began writing their own songs, they realized that they needed to add another singer. They held auditions and discovered Janie "Bob" Scott, who joined the group and helped to polish their performances.

The name Bobs is of uncertain origin. It might be an acronym for Best of Breed, which is an award given out at dog shows for the overall winner of the show. Or it might be a short version of the Oral Bobs. Or it might be something else. In any case, although none of the singers is actually named Bob, all use Bob for a middle name.

Kaleidoscope Records in San Francisco produced their first album, *The Bobs*. They got a Grammy nomination for their version of "Helter Skelter," which also won a Contemporary A Cappella Recording Award (CARA) in 1996. Their award was presented with the following comments: "Rather than translating instrumental parts to voices or relying on clichéd syllables and voicings, Gunnar and Richard created a new vocabulary of sounds and textures. The arrangement deconstructs the song line by line, transforming the Beatles classic into an a cappella, post-modern performance art piece." This recognition helped launch a national tour; they also received exposure on radio and television, and embarked on tours across the U.S. and Europe, including performances at major music festivals. They have since won numerous CARA awards.

Since their early success, the Bobs have written songs on many odd and witty topics. These include cattle farming on the moon, doing laundry, Watergate villains, graffiti, security guards at shopping malls, cats who want to conquer the world, tattoos, spontaneous human combustion, heart transplants, bus drivers, violence at the post office, and other amusing curiosities. Furthermore, their a cappella arrangements are very unusual. Some have called their performances a cross between the Barenaked Ladies and the Manhattan Transfer.

While most of their music is a cappella, they have included toy drums, technology that distorts their voices, a piano, clapping, and occasional rock band accompaniment. But since they formed in 1981 they have primarily sung a cappella music. While never a widespread commercial success, they have developed a healthy cult following that has kept them performing and recording for over 25 years. Their fans rewarded them by attending several concerts in 2006 to celebrate the 25th Anniversary of the Bobs, in which seven of the eight singers from the band's history performed. A documentary film about their first quarter-century together, *Sign My Snarling Movie: 25 Years of the Bobs*, was released in 2007.

The Bobs have not been content simply with singing. They have also worked with dance companies. They wrote a series of songs, "The Laundry Cycle," for the Oberlin Dance Collective in 1987. At around the same time they met the dance troupe named Momix, later known as ISO. Their collaboration was known for its improvisation and creativity. This work attracted the attention of the Lincoln Center, which resulted in a show on public television and recognition in the Smithsonian Institute's Museum of American History. They have also provided the majority of the soundtrack for the 1996 film *For Better or Worse*, and during the televised Emmy Award program, they performed a medley of television themes with former *Seinfeld* co-star Jason Alexander.

The band's membership has completely turned over since the original quartet. Co-founder Gunnar "Bob" Madsen retired in 1990, and was replaced by Joe "Bob" Finetti for a thirteen-year run with the band. Other changes in personnel occurred as well. The group has therefore both evolved and remained true to its core principles of performing musically adroit yet wacky lyrics, sound effects, and arrangements for a highly entertaining effect. The *Bergen (NJ) Record/Home News Tribune* has described the Bobs as "One of the most entertaining acts on the live circuit today."

Original members:

Matthew "Bob" Stull	Richard "Bob" Greene
Gunnar "Bob" Madsen	Janie "Bob" Scott

In-between members:

Lori "Bob" Rivera	Joe "Bob" Finetti

Current members:

Richard "Bob" Greene	Amy "Bob" Engelhardt
Matthew "Bob" Stull	Dan "Bob" Schumacher

Who Are the Persuasions?

The Persuasions
Official website: www.thepersuasions.net

The Persuasions are an a cappella singing group that formed in Brooklyn in 1966. The group has had a very stable membership over the years, although the personnel have changed as the band has aged (and in one case, died). Jerry Lawson, who left the group in 2003 to do charitable work and perform solo, was a founding member and sang lead vocals for over four decades. Second tenor "Sweet" Joe Russell has sung the high range of the arrangements for most of the group's history, although he took a leave of absence due to illness at one point and presently is the Persuasions' lead singer. Jimmy Hayes has been a stalwart as the group's bass singer and has occasionally sung lead vocals on songs such as "Sixty Minute Man." Jayotis Washington sings tenor and occasional lead and has also been with the group since its founding, with a brief departure from which he returned. Herbert "Tuobo" Rhodes, an original Persuasion who sang harmonies in the baritone range, died in 1988 while the band was touring.

During the core members' absences from the band, others have filled their roles in the group's harmonies. Temporary Persuasions have included Bernard Jones, Willie C. Daniels, and Beverly Rohlehr, the band's only female member, who briefly filled in for Joe Russell and sang high harmonies. Ray Sanders and Reggie Moore (who replaced Jerry Lawson) have joined the band on a permanent basis, rounding out the remaining original members Jayotis Washington, Jimmy Hayes, and Joe Russell. For the most part the Persuasions have included five singers, but have toured and recorded albums with four during various members' leaves of absence from the band and following Toubo Rhodes' death.

The Persuasions have released about twenty albums over the course of their 45+ year history and have performed on stages all over the world. They have performed concerts on their own and have also opened for Frank Zappa and the Mothers of Invention, Joni Mitchell, Ray Charles, Bill Cosby, Richard Pryor, and other major stars. And early in their careers, Roseanne Barr and Bruce Springsteen opened for the Persuasions. They have also recorded and performed with a diverse array of musicians, including Stevie Wonder, Bette Midler, Liza Minelli, Van Morrison, Lou Reed, Gladys Knight, Patti LaBelle, Little Richard, Nancy Wilson, the Neville Brothers, Country Joe McDonald, B.B. King, and Paul Simon. Not only have they kept distinguished company, they have performed at levels at least as high as those of their friends and collaborators.

The Persuasions' music is grounded in gospel, soul, doo-wop, and rhythm & blues music, although they have also performed music from other genres. They have written little music of their own, choosing instead to interpret songs from other composers' catalogues. Their songs have come from the African American church, Motown, soul artists such as Sam Cooke (their most important influence), Elvis Presley, and others. Even when the song they sing was originally not soulful, their performance of it always is. More recently they have dedicated whole albums to the music of significant artists, including CDs featuring the music of the Beatles, Frank Zappa, U2, and the Grateful Dead. They have also released albums centering on gospel music and children's songs. In every case their music is inspired, soulful, and filled with energy and humor.

The Persuasions are considered by many to be the epitome of a cappella music, especially in the area of doo-wop, soul, and gospel-inspired music. Many groups list them among their most important influences, including Take 6, the Nylons, Rockapella, and Boys II Men. In many ways they are responsible for the survival of a cappella music outside the confines of barbershops and college choral groups. The secret to their success is that they have not sold out. They did record one album with musical accompaniment but abandoned the experiment and returned to their roots for the remainder of their history. No matter what the source of their music—Rodgers and Hammerstein, Bob Dylan, Clyde McPhatter, or children's songs—they infuse the music with their wit, charm, energy, and soaring harmonies. They have taken songs from across the musical spectrum and reinvented them as pure Persuasions creations.

In the 1990s Persuasions admirer Fred Parnes produced the documentary film *Spread the Word: The Persuasions Sing A Cappella*, which has been warmly embraced by the Persuasions' many admirers. Their music has appeared in film soundtracks as diverse as *Joe Versus the Volcano*, *The Heartbreak Kid*, *Streets of Gold*, and *E.T. the Extraterrestrial*. They have also appeared on several television specials, including Spike Lee's *Do It A Cappella* (in which they were described as "the godfathers of a cappella") and the public television special *Music of the Late Kurt Weill*. They have additionally sung on *Good Morning America*, the *Today Show*, the *Tonight Show*, *Saturday Night Live!*, and *Late Night with Conan O'Brien*.

The Persuasions keep on keepin' on, weathering changes in personnel and the ever fickle public taste in music. They have endured because of their love for their work and their talent in choosing material, arranging it, and singing it with gusto. They are truly the Godfathers of A Cappella, the Kings of A Cappella, and every other accolade bestowed upon them since the early 1960s. May they sing forever.

Using the notes they have taken, the members of each group explain to the others which performance they have decided to see. As students comment on or question their classmates' thinking (different groups will most likely have developed different procedures for using their source material), each group has an opportunity to rethink and revise its decision before going their separate ways to write their papers.

EPISODE 6.2

A hallmark of a structured process approach is that students often *develop procedures inductively*. Rather than modeling a way to do things, teachers develop activities that require problem-framing and problem-solving discussions through which students develop procedures and approaches appropriate to the task. Groups of students who have worked together then talk with other groups and share their thinking about the task, thus expanding everyone's ideas.

Extensions

1. Reemploy some of the processes used in previous stages and episodes of the sequence. For instance, if students have trouble generating content, conduct additional small-group sessions devoted to coming up with ideas. Or have students individually write about ideas they have produced as a group. Or have groups give and receive additional peer feedback before writing final drafts.

2. If a comparison and contrast essay appears on a state- or districtwide writing test, have students write comparison and contrast essays on topics and under conditions that mimic those on the test.

3. Feature comparison and contrast essays in a conceptual unit (see Smagorinsky 2008 and www.coe.uga.edu/~smago/VirtualLibrary/Unit_Outlines.htm) centered on a theme (e.g., gender roles), genre (e.g., allegory), archetype (e.g., the folk hero), reading strategy (e.g., understanding point of view), single author's works (e.g., the works of Alice Walker), movement (e.g., the Black Arts Movement), period (e.g., the British Restoration), or region (e.g., the authors of Arizona). Students can compare and contrast:

   - Authors within a category (e.g., Haki Madhubuti and Nikki Giovanni, Jack Kerouac and Allen Ginsberg).

   - Characters within a work (e.g., Huck Finn and Tom Sawyer, Lord and Lady Macbeth). "Heroes" (on the next page) is an example of a comparison/contrast essay on Lancelot and King Arthur from Angela's classroom.

- Characters in related texts (e.g., Tartuffe and Volpone, Ozymandius and Miniver Cheevy).

- Songs related to unit concepts (e.g., in a unit on "the journey," Johnny Clegg and Savuka's "Spirit Is the Journey" and Joni Mitchell's "Woodstock"; in a unit on discrimination, Harry Belafonte's "Kwela (Listen to the Man)" and the Dave Matthews Band's "Cry Freedom").

- Film and literary versions of the same text (e.g., the film and graphic novel versions of *V for Vendetta*; *Romeo and Juliet* and *West Side Story*).

- Different perspectives on the same concept or event (e.g., Michael Franti and Spearhead's "Light Up Ya Lighter" and Toby Keith's "Courtesy of the Red, White, & Blue (The Angry American)."

Fernando's Essay: Heroes

A hero is a person that helps other people. Heroes are strong, brave, loyal, and smart. A real hero doesn't need to have super powers. They just need to help and do good for their people and their city. Lancelot is more of a hero than Arthur.

King Arthur was a strong leader, generous, and in love. For example, he was a strong leader because he fought at the end instead of obeying Malagant and showed pride to his people. He also led his men into fighting Malagant's army. He was generous by letting Lancelot join and become a knight at the round table. This shows that he's willing to trust others and he wants protection from a brave knight. King Arthur is in love with Guinevere because he sends a lot of his men to get her. They will bring her back to Camelot so Arthur can marry her. As you can see, King Arthur could be a good hero because he's strong, generous, but he's not as good as Lancelot.

Lancelot is brave, loyal, and is in love with Guinevere. For example, he's brave because he doesn't fear death and he likes to fight a lot. He also fights 10 men at the same time and he kills them all and he's not afraid of anyone or anything. He's also loyal because he accepted King Arthur's invitation and joined the round table to protect his king. Also, when Malagant attacked, he protected his city by killing about 50 men. Lancelot is in love with Guinevere because he went after Guinevere when she was kidnapped by Malagant and saves her. He also kept pursuing her after she rejected him. In the end, Lancelot is more of a hero because he has all of a hero's characteristics.

Lancelot is more of a hero than Arthur. They both have some hero characteristics. Heroes can have flaws, but they have to fight it and not lose. We know that nobody is perfect, so heroes can have flaws. We need heroes because they make the world a better and safer place to live.

What Makes This Sequence a Structured Process Approach?

This sequence of activities illustrates many features of a structured process approach. Angela has worked hard outside class assembling materials for students to compare and contrast. The three essays comparing and contrasting two breakfast cereals and the descriptions of two *a cappella* singing groups were written outside class, after some Internet sleuthing. In class, however, the students do the work as they talk and write about the materials provided.

The activities scaffold students' progression through a series of increasingly complex tasks, beginning with topics volunteered by the students and concluding with unfamiliar topics requiring the students to consult source material. Always, however, the students are able to base their thinking and writing on concrete data; they do not fabricate the content of their writing.

The activities are highly social, with students involved in whole-group and small-group discussions at every stage of the instruction. These discussions allow the students to try out ideas and engage in exploratory talk through which new insights may develop. Their initial efforts at composing are done collaboratively; students get immediate feedback on their efforts and receive help shaping their understanding of the topic and expressing their beliefs.

The emphasis throughout is on learning procedures for comparing and contrasting. Although every group doesn't necessarily develop identical procedures, they are introduced to other groups' processes and can borrow those procedures. The language lesson focuses on procedures as well; students combine sentences to create complex sentences juxtaposing two ideas. This approach is therefore *generative* in that students manipulate the language into their own sentence constructions; in contrast, most textbook grammar lessons we have seen simply require students to recognize and repair errors in someone else's writing.

Ultimately, the emphasis on procedures gives students a tool kit for expanding their options when writing comparison and contrast essays. Appropriate extensions help students reapply these procedures, thus reinforcing their understanding of how to use them as they develop as writers.

Questions for Reflection

1. What topics from the local community would make appropriate subjects for students to compare and contrast?

2. What issues are involved in comparing and contrasting for students of different ages, grade levels, literacy levels, English proficiency levels, cultural backgrounds, and other factors?

3. How can students' background cultural knowledge be used as a bridge to conventional school knowledge in the area of comparing and contrasting?

4. How can comparing and contrasting fit easily with the demands of the existing literature, language, and writing curricula?

5. For what authentic purposes can students be taught how to compare and contrast effectively through writing?

6. In what ways can comparison and contrast writing instruction be tied to writing assessment so as not to disrupt the continuity of instruction?

7. How can the assessment of students' comparison and contrast writing be responsive to differences in their initial abilities to write such essays?

8. In what ways can technology be incorporated into comparison and contrast writing instruction?

9. What other genres of expression are available to enhance students' comparison and contrast composing (e.g., art, music, oral speech, etc.) for different audiences and purposes?

10. In what ways can comparison and contrast writing help students learn strategies for engaging in other sorts of writing tasks?

CHAPTER

7

Teaching
Extended Definition
Essays

Early one fall, Betsy Kahn and the other teachers in her school met to select students for membership in the National Honor Society. They rated students in three areas—character, leadership, and service—based on criteria provided by the Society. For example, *leadership* was defined as "being resourceful," "promoting school activities," and "exemplifying positive attitudes about life." The criteria further specified that "leadership experiences can be drawn from school or community activities while working with or for others."

The group extended these defining criteria as they discussed the students on the nomination list. For example, one student held an important office in the student council, something that would seemingly qualify her as a leader. However, this student often made commitments she didn't keep (e.g., saying she would make table decorations for the homecoming dance and then not following through). So the evaluating teachers added another leadership criterion: fulfilling one's responsibilities and commitments to a group or organization.

Another student had initiated a protest against a school policy that only seniors who had passed the state tests their junior year would be exempt from final exams. The key factor here was that the student had acted in a mature and appropriate manner: gathering signatures on a petition, getting the issue on a school board meeting agenda, and speaking effectively at the meeting. The teachers also established limits by developing a contrasting example: had the student encouraged students to boycott classes or staged a walkout, his leadership could be questioned.

These teachers were developing an extended definition of *leadership*: formulating more explicit and more detailed *criteria* than the ones provided. The teachers drew on what they knew about the candidates to help formulate the criteria by which they would make their judgment, and the candidates were *examples* of meeting or falling short of the qualities the criteria called for. To explain why a candidate did or did not illustrate a criterion, the teachers provided a *warrant*, Toulmin's (1958) term for an explanation of how an example does or does not serve as evidence in support of a claim.

Students are often faced with developing an extended definition of a concept. Is a certain literary character acting courageously? Who should be given the Student Government Leadership Award? Who should be elected to the homecoming court? Does freedom of the press allow students to criticize the school administration in the student newspaper? When is failure to credit a source an honest mistake and when it is plagiarism?

Our larger society faces similar dilemmas. Is the federal rescue of failed industries an act of socialism? Does helping transport dogs to a dog-fighting arena constitute cruelty to animals? Is sharing a confidence with others the act of a friend? Is a sculpture depicting something offensive to a portion of the public a work of art? Is someone speaking truth to power when his critique brings him fame and fortune?

Students need to learn how to take complex concepts, define them using clear and unambiguous criteria, and identify behavior that does and does not illustrate each criterion (see Johannessen et al. 1982).

Task Analysis

The process of creating an extended definition is complex. How can teachers design instruction to scaffold students' ability to write extended definitions? First we need to identify the procedures people go through in developing an extended definition:

- Identify a defining problem or target concept.

- Generate *examples*, either real or hypothetical.

- Formulate *criteria*.

- Relate examples to criteria.

- Analyze borderline cases.

- Clarify the limits of a term or concept through *contrasting examples*.

- Explain examples and contrasting examples by means of a *warrant*.

The process may be linear—following the steps in this exact order—or recursive—moving from formulating criteria to relating examples to the criteria to analyzing borderline cases back to reformulating criteria or formulating additional criteria, and so forth.

Next we need to design activities through which students use an accessible set of materials to define abstract concepts by generating *criteria*; providing supporting *examples* that meet each criterion, as well as *contrasting examples* that do not; and justifying the examples using *warrants*. Students learning to write extended definitions for the first time need separate instruction in each of these procedures, instruction that begins with accessible materials and problems and gradually leads them through more complex concepts and definitions.

Stage 1. Gateway Activity: Defining a Hero

Students often have trouble grasping what criteria are. One way to begin is to give students a set of criteria and have them, first as a class and then in small groups, determine whether examples fulfill the criteria or not.

Most students are intrigued by the Carnegie Hero Award, awarded by the Carnegie Hero Fund Commission to "a civilian who voluntarily risks his or her own life, knowingly, to an extraordinary degree while saving or attempting to save the life of another person" (www.carnegiehero.org). The criteria are:

- The person being rescued must clearly be in danger of losing his or her life.

- The rescue must be one in which no measure of responsibility exists between the rescuer and the rescued.

- The awardee must be a civilian acting voluntarily (not on active duty in the armed services or on a police or firefighting force).

- Those whose regular jobs require them to perform such acts are not eligible unless the rescues are clearly beyond the line of duty.

- A person is not eligible if he or she is saving the life of an immediate family member, except in cases of outstanding heroism where the rescuer loses his or her life or is severely injured.

- The rescuer must risk his or her own life to an extraordinary degree.

- The rescuer must comprehend the risks involved (not be too young or otherwise unable to understand the potential consequences).

The Carnegie Hero website also includes profiles of those who have received the medal. Here's the story of winner Curtis Dawson, from Astoria, Oregon:

> Curtis Dawson helped to rescue David M. Schmelzer from drowning, Astoria, Oregon, December 3, 2005. Schmelzer, 67, was the captain of a tugboat that was towing a barge on the Columbia River at night. The tugboat capsized in the swift ebb-tide current and floated upside down and partially submerged. Dawson, 47, assistant engineer, was working as a deckhand on the barge and witnessed the accident. Minutes later, he saw Schmelzer, unconscious, float toward the surface of the water alongside the barge. Although both the barge and the tugboat were then adrift, Dawson, fully attired, jumped five feet down into the river, despite the coldness of the water and limited visibility in the darkness. He swam to Schmelzer, grasped his jacket, and pulled his head above water. Realizing that they were being carried away from the barge, Dawson started to swim back to it, Schmelzer in tow. A deckhand threw a rope to Dawson and pulled the men to the side of the barge. With another man holding him, the deckhand leaned over the side of the barge, grasped Schmelzer, and with others worked with Dawson for several minutes to lift him to the barge deck. Cold and becoming numb, Dawson climbed and was aided from the water back to the deck. A bar pilot helicopter responded soon and lowered a sling that was used to lift Schmelzer from the water. He was taken ashore and then to the hospital, where he was admitted for treatment. Dawson also was taken to the hospital, where he was treated for cold-water immersion. Both men recovered.

EPISODE 1.1   Give students a copy of the criteria for the Carnegie Hero Award and the description of the actions of Curtis Dawson, but don't reveal whether Dawson received the award. In a whole-class discussion, have students determine whether or not Dawson meets each of the criteria for the award, citing evidence from the provided information.

EPISODE 1.2   Give students a less clear-cut case—a *borderline example* (see Figure 7–1)—to debate without your guidance and feedback. Have them, in groups of three or four, discuss whether Roger Terrapin meets each criterion for the Carnegie Hero Award and why he is or is not as worthy as Curtis Dawson. Discussions will tend to focus on whether Terrapin risked his own life to an extraordinary degree, the most contestable criterion. Some may argue that his Navy training made the rescue not so extraordinary. Also, the water was probably

Figure 7–1. Carnegie Hero Award Candidate

Roger Terrapin lives in a suburb of Memphis, Tennessee, where he makes his living as a mail carrier. He spent 12 years in the Navy and received extensive training as a Navy SEAL in diving and underwater rescue. On a beautiful September afternoon, Michael and Mary Landlock were driving home from the hospital where Michael is a dialysis patient. They were approaching a stop sign when their brakes failed. To avoid hitting any cars, Michael drove up onto the sidewalk and into a retention pond. Terrapin saw the truck drive into the pond. The Landlocks' truck was sinking fast, so Terrapin left his car in traffic, ran down the bank, and dove into the water. Mary rolled down her window, and Mr. Terrapin was easily able to pull her out and pull her to the bank about 45 feet away. Two other rescuers were struggling to get Michael Landlock out of the car. They were not able to help him, but Terrapin's Navy days of water rescue prepared him well. The retention pond was not deep—around 12 feet—however, the sinking truck's undertow was pulling him down. He grabbed Landlock and jerked him three or four times, finally releasing him from the vehicle before it completely submerged. With the couple safely on shore, Terrapin left for home without giving anyone his name.

not dangerously cold and the pond was not particularly deep or hazardous. On the other hand, the truck was creating an undertow. Have groups report back to their classmates and debate the issues further. This prompts students to think critically about the meaning of the criteria and recognize different viewpoints, reasoning, and evidence.

Stage 2. Learning Procedures for Formulating Criteria

Now that students understand how criteria function in an extended definition, have them create criteria themselves in a new problem based on the relatively familiar concept of dishonesty.

Start by giving students a set of scenarios that may or may not be examples of dishonesty (see Figure 7–2). Have them, in groups of three or four, discuss each of the scenarios and develop a set of criteria for defining dishonesty. Talking through their ideas in this relatively nonthreatening setting, they can

EPISODE 2.1

Figure 7–2. Honest or Dishonest?

After discussing each of these scenarios, create a set of criteria for determining whether a person has acted *dishonestly*.

1. Alfonzo finds a twenty-dollar bill lying on the sidewalk in a residential area. No one is around at the time. Alfonzo keeps the money. Is he honest? Dishonest? Explain why.

2. Gerald finds a briefcase hidden under some bushes in a residential area. Inside the briefcase are many bundles of hundred-dollar bills. Gerald takes the brief-case home and plans to keep the money. Is he being honest? Dishonest? Explain why.

3. Adriana's neighbor gets a new hairstyle. Adriana doesn't particularly like the new look, but when her neighbor asks her opinion, she tells her, "You look very nice," because she doesn't want to hurt her feelings. Is she honest? Dishonest? Explain.

4. Sareena drove her parents' car to the mall by herself for the first time. She got a speeding ticket on the way home. When she returned home, her parents asked how everything had gone. She decided not to tell her parents about the ticket and said, "Okay; everything was fine." Is she honest? Dishonest? Explain.

5. Simon lost his copy of *The Adventures of Huckleberry Finn* that he needed for class. His friend suggested that he go to the lost and found and look for a copy without any name in it. Simon did just that and found a book, which he then kept. Is he being honest? Dishonest? Explain.

6. Erika's friend told her that outside the cafeteria there were coolers with sodas that were free for students. Erika told several of her friends, who each went and got a soda. Erika's friend knew the sodas were not free but were for a club fundraiser. Is Erika honest? Dishonest? Explain.

7. Tom's friend told him that in the school media center there were some boxes of DVDs of current movies in the back corner and that the librarian said it was okay to take any of them he wanted. Tom went into the media center and found the boxes of new DVDs. No one was around, so he took three of them. Tom's friend made up the whole story, and the DVDs belonged to the school. Is Tom being honest? Dishonest? Explain.

8. Martina thinks the company's pens at the clothing store where she works are really cool. Without asking her boss if it's all right, she takes three of them home with her and gives two of them to her friends. Is she being honest? Dishonest? Explain.

experiment with ideas that may or may not pan out without fear of being "wrong." They also get immediate feedback, which channels their thinking toward a culturally appropriate definition.

Then ask them to share their ideas in a whole-class discussion. Typically, students come up with criteria like these for dishonesty:

- A person twists, distorts, or covers up the truth in some way.

- The twisting, distorting, or covering up of the truth is done intentionally.

- The person knows he or she is doing something wrong.

- There exists a possibility of finding the truth, the rightful owner, or other conscientious solution.

- There is an intention to deceive, cheat, or deprive someone of something rightfully his or hers.

- The person does not take responsibility for looking into suspicious, inauthentic, or unjust aspects of the situation.

Students often point out how the Alfonzo scenario contrasts with the Gerald scenario. They argue that there is no way Alfonzo can find the rightful owner of the money but that Gerald has a responsibility to turn in the money to the police, who could possibly find the rightful owner. They also contrast Erika with Tom. Tom should have known the situation was fishy and checked with the media center director to be sure he could take the DVDs; there were no red flags in Erika's case—there is no reason for her not to believe her friend, so taking the soda is an honest mistake. (Of course, if Erika's friend had a history of telling Erika things that weren't true, then Erika's honesty would be in question.)

As the students defend their interpretations of the examples, they develop the rudiments of warrants that explain the relation between a claim and an example.

Ask students to select a scenario from Figure 7–2 and create a contrasting example for it, working individually, in small groups, or as a class, depending on how well they understand the idea and how much support they need. Have them read their contrasting example to the class, tell how it differs from the original scenario, and explain how it clarifies one of the criteria.

EPISODE 2.2

To help students turn their discussion and thinking about the scenarios into extended definition essays, provide a few sample paragraphs for them to evaluate and eventually revise (see the activity in Figure 7–3).

EPISODE 2.3

Figure 7–3. Paragraphs on Honesty

Directions: Read each of the three paragraphs. What are the strengths and weaknesses of each? What, if anything, is missing or confusing? Answer the following questions as you analyze each paragraph.

1. Does the paragraph present a clearly stated criterion for dishonesty? If so, what is it?

2. Does the paragraph include a specific example to illustrate or explain the criterion? Explain.

3. Does the writer explain how or why the example fulfills the criterion? Explain.

4. Does the writer include a contrasting example to set limits? Explain.

5. Choose the paragraph that is the weakest and revise it to make it more effective.

Paragraph A

Dishonesty involves twisting, distorting, or covering up the truth. For example, Sareena drove her parents' car to the mall by herself for the first time. She got a speeding ticket on the way home. When she returned home, her parents asked how everything had gone. She decided not to tell her parents about the ticket and said, "Okay; everything was fine."

Paragraph B

What if someone tells her neighbor a "white lie" to protect her feelings? Is that being dishonest? Let's say the neighbor gets a new hairstyle that she is really excited about and the other neighbor tells her that it looks nice even though she doesn't particularly like it. It would be impolite and hurtful to say that you don't like the person's haircut. It isn't wrong to be polite.

Paragraph C

Imagine that a person finds a twenty-dollar bill lying on the sidewalk. No one is in sight. Would it be dishonest to keep the twenty-dollar bill? In this case, keeping the bill would not be dishonest. There is basically no way that the person can find the owner. If he leaves the bill on the walk, it will most likely be blown away or picked up by someone else. Turning it in to the police wouldn't accomplish anything either. The police couldn't find the owner. Dishonesty involves intentionally deceiving or cheating someone out of something, and in this case no one has been intentionally deceived or cheated. The person would have a clear conscience taking the money. If, on the other hand, the person found a bag full of thousands of dollars left in the bushes, it would be dishonest to try to keep it. It would be something the person would have to hide from others. If the police knew about it, they would require the person to turn it over to them. If you have to hide your actions, it is a sign that you're not being honest.

Stage 3. Language Lesson: Learning Procedures for Providing Warrants

While instruction in argumentation typically includes attention to claims and examples, warrants are often overlooked. When claims and examples are simply juxtaposed—without an explanation of how the example provides evidence for the claim—the resulting argument can be specious (Hillocks 2002). To help students produce warrants, introduce them to connective terms that signal the presence of a warrant and have them complete an exercise in which they must explain claims and examples in terms of one another. A minilesson for this purpose is provided in Figure 7–4.

Figure 7–4. Minilesson on Introducing Warrants

A *warrant* is a statement that explains why a specific example provides evidence in support of a criterion or other sort of claim. Often, a warrant is introduced by words that are synonymous with *because*. These words and phrases include:

due to	inasmuch as
for the reason that	owing to
in light of	since
in that	through
in view of the fact that	whereas

Here are some ways in which you might illustrate a criterion with an example/contrasting example and use one of these words to introduce a warrant that explains why it is appropriate for the criterion or does not meet the criterion. (The criteria are those required of recipients of the Carnegie Hero Award.)

Criterion: The rescuer must risk his or her own life to an extraordinary degree.

Example: Leila did not know how to swim when she jumped into the rapids to save Randy's life.

Warrant: *Because* Leila might have drowned by attempting to rescue Randy, and the rapids made swimming dangerous even for an experienced swimmer, Leila was heroic for jumping into the river.

(continues)

Figure 7–4. Minilesson on Introducing Warrants *(continued)*

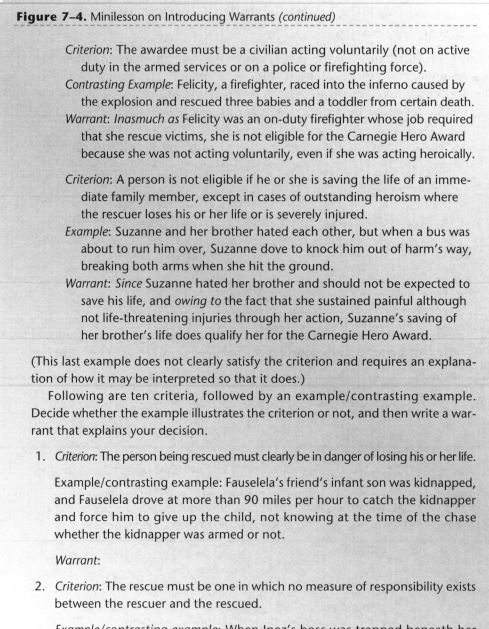

Criterion: The awardee must be a civilian acting voluntarily (not on active duty in the armed services or on a police or firefighting force).

Contrasting Example: Felicity, a firefighter, raced into the inferno caused by the explosion and rescued three babies and a toddler from certain death.

Warrant: *Inasmuch as* Felicity was an on-duty firefighter whose job required that she rescue victims, she is not eligible for the Carnegie Hero Award because she was not acting voluntarily, even if she was acting heroically.

Criterion: A person is not eligible if he or she is saving the life of an immediate family member, except in cases of outstanding heroism where the rescuer loses his or her life or is severely injured.

Example: Suzanne and her brother hated each other, but when a bus was about to run him over, Suzanne dove to knock him out of harm's way, breaking both arms when she hit the ground.

Warrant: *Since* Suzanne hated her brother and should not be expected to save his life, and *owing to* the fact that she sustained painful although not life-threatening injuries through her action, Suzanne's saving of her brother's life does qualify her for the Carnegie Hero Award.

(This last example does not clearly satisfy the criterion and requires an explanation of how it may be interpreted so that it does.)

Following are ten criteria, followed by an example/contrasting example. Decide whether the example illustrates the criterion or not, and then write a warrant that explains your decision.

1. *Criterion*: The person being rescued must clearly be in danger of losing his or her life.

   Example/contrasting example: Fauselela's friend's infant son was kidnapped, and Fauselela drove at more than 90 miles per hour to catch the kidnapper and force him to give up the child, not knowing at the time of the chase whether the kidnapper was armed or not.

   Warrant:

2. *Criterion*: The rescue must be one in which no measure of responsibility exists between the rescuer and the rescued.

   Example/contrasting example: When Inez's boss was trapped beneath her massive oak desk following the earthquake, Inez lifted the desk and helped her out of the building, even with the threat of aftershocks present.

   Warrant:

(continues)

Figure 7–4. Minilesson on Introducing Warrants *(continued)*

3. *Criterion*: The awardee must be a civilian acting voluntarily (not on active duty in the armed services or on a police or firefighting force).

   Example/contrasting example: Preston, an off-duty volunteer firefighter, went into a burning vehicle following a car crash and rescued the injured victim from certain death.

   Warrant:

4. *Criterion*: Those whose regular jobs require them to perform such acts are not eligible unless the rescues are clearly beyond the line of duty.

   Example/contrasting example: Yao, a lifeguard, swam a quarter of a mile out into the ocean as a hurricane approached to rescue a boat-wreck survivor who was hanging on to a floating plank.

   Warrant:

5. *Criterion*: A person is not eligible if he or she is saving the life of an immediate family member, except in cases of outstanding heroism where the rescuer loses his or her life or is severely injured.

   Example/contrasting example: Juaniqua dove into swirling waters to rescue Wags, her beloved family dog of thirteen years, drowning in the process but saving Wags' life.

   Warrant:

6. *Criterion*: The rescuer must risk his or her own life to an extraordinary degree.

   Example/contrasting example: When D'Andre saw a stranger climb over the fence of the lion's enclosure at the zoo, he leaped the fence, grabbed her, and dragged her back to safety before the lions noticed that she had entered their habitat.

   Warrant:

7. *Criterion*: The rescuer must comprehend the risks involved (not be too young or otherwise unable to understand the potential consequences).

   Example/contrasting example: When Hisako's friend Fredo said to the menacing intruder who claimed to have a gun in his pocket, "Your mama is so dumb she spent a half hour looking at an orange juice box because it said 'concentrate,'" Hisako stepped between them and ordered the intruder to leave.

   Warrant:

(continues)

Figure 7–4. Minilesson on Introducing Warrants *(continued)*

8. *Criterion*: A person is not eligible if he or she is saving the life of an immediate family member, except in cases of outstanding heroism where the rescuer loses his or her life or is severely injured.

   Example/contrasting example: Pierre dove off a 100-foot cliff into the sea to rescue his drowning stepsister Porchia, hitting his head on the coral reef below and requiring reconstructive facial surgery after saving her life.

   Warrant:

9. *Criterion*: The rescuer must risk his or her own life to an extraordinary degree.

   Example/contrasting example: When the trapped and heavily armed bank robbers told Henrique that they would let their hostage go if he agreed to take her place, he agreed.

   Warrant:

10. *Criterion*: Those whose regular jobs require them to perform such acts are not eligible unless the rescues are clearly beyond the line of duty.

    Example/contrasting example: Detective Randolph, while driving to her karate class on her way home from her shift, saw a gang beating up a young man and single-handedly disarmed, disabled, and handcuffed all five of the alleged perpetrators.

    Warrant:

Stage 4. Applying Knowledge of Procedures in Collaborative Writing

By writing a composition in small groups, students experience the support of their peers before putting their ideas into writing independently. Episodes 4.1a and 4.1b are alternative activities; students who struggle with one will benefit from doing both.

EPISODE 4.1a   Ask students in small groups to write an extended definition of *dishonesty* using the scenarios in Figure 7–2 as a basis for their thinking. Suggest they use the following format (or one like it) to help them organize their composition:

- *First paragraph: introduction.* Introduce the concept/problem, explaining why it's important to define the concept or why it is difficult in some cases to define the concept.

- *Second paragraph: first criterion.*

  - Explain the criterion as clearly as possible.

  - Give an example that fulfills the criterion.

  - Provide a warrant explaining how the example fulfills the criterion.

  - Give a contrasting example.

  - Provide a warrant explaining how the contrasting example clarifies the limits of the criterion.

- *Each subsequent body paragraph.* Explain, illustrate, and warrant each additional criterion.

- *Final paragraph: conclusion.*

Give students Washington Irving's short story "The Adventure of the Mason" (see www.42opus.com/v8n1/the-adventure-of-the-mason). In the story, a poor mason, who is described as "honest" and "a good Christian," is roused from sleep one night by a priest. The priest blindfolds him and leads him on a circuitous route to a house. Once inside the house, the priest removes the blindfold. He pays the mason generously for building a small brick vault within an interior courtyard—a vault suitable for hiding jars full of money. After completing the work, the mason is blindfolded again and led back home.

EPISODE 4.1b

Some years pass, and a landlord hires the mason to repair an old house of his that has fallen into decay. The house is said to be haunted by the sound of "the clinking of gold all night in the chamber where the former owner had slept." Once inside the house, the mason recognizes it as the house in which he had built a vault to hide jars of money. When he inquires about the former owner of the house, the new owner tells him it had belonged to a "miserly priest" who was said to be "immensely rich." It was thought that he would leave all his treasures to the church. The priest died suddenly, and when all the priests and friars came to take possession of the wealth, they could find nothing.

The mason agrees to live in the house and repair it. The narrator states, "The offer of the honest mason was gladly accepted. . . . By little and little he restored it to its former state; the clinking of gold was no more heard at night in the chamber of the defunct priest, but began to be heard by day in the pocket of the living mason."

Ask the students whether the "honest mason" is truly honest. Have them, in small groups, use the criteria for dishonesty they have developed as the basis for a composition arguing whether or not the mason is dishonest. Suggest the following organization:

- *First paragraph: introduction.* Introduce the short story and the questions it raises about the mason's honesty. State a position concerning whether the mason is dishonest.

- *Second paragraph: first criterion fulfilled, if there is one.*

  - Explain the first criterion as clearly as possible.

  - Give an example that meets the criterion.

  - Provide a warrant explaining how the example meets the criterion.

- *Subsequent body paragraphs.* Explain, illustrate, and warrant each additional criterion that is fulfilled by the character, if there are any.

- *Next body paragraph: first criterion NOT fulfilled, if there is one.*

- *Subsequent body paragraphs.* Explain, illustrate, and warrant each additional criterion, if any, NOT fulfilled by the character.

- *Final paragraph: conclusion.*

Monitor the students' work, reminding them to explicitly state and explain each of the criteria for dishonesty and to use specific scenarios or examples from the story.

EPISODE 4.2 Post the compositions on a class bulletin board, website, or wiki for the rest of the class to read. Review the criteria for an effective composition and then have students determine the strengths of each and make suggestions for improvement. The example composition, "A Dishonest Man," has strengths and weaknesses that are fairly typical of student writing. The student does a good job of stating each criterion and providing examples from the story showing how the mason meets it. However, she sometimes has difficulty stating the criteria clearly and fluently.

A Dishonest Man, by Jessica

Washington Irving's tale "The Adventure of the Mason" focuses on a mason who is a very poor person who will do anything to put food on the table for his family. One day a wealthy Priest comes to the mason's door and asks if he would help him with a job and is willing to pay him. The job was to help bury the Priests money in his house. A few years later a wealthy landowner asks the mason to help renovate the house which happened to be the old priest's house. The mason being a "Good Samaritan" decides to take the house off the man's hands without telling him that there was millions of dollars there. The mason became one of the richest men in Granada. The story proposes a question is the mason honest or dishonest? Dishonesty is a disposition to lie, cheat, or steal. There are four main criteria to meet to be a dishonest person which are someone must be intentional, done knowingly, know that what you're doing is wrong; twist or distort or cover up the truth in some way; there exists a possibility to find the rightful owner, the truth, etc.; and a person has the intention to deceive, cheat, or deprive someone of something rightfully his or hers. The mason portrays a dishonest person by fulfilling all of these aspects.

One of the criteria to be classified as a dishonest person is to twist, distort, cover up the truth in some way. The wealthy landlord had no idea about the hidden money on his property. "Enough," said the mason sturdily, "let me live in your house rent-free until some better tenant present, and I will engage to put it in repair, and to quiet the troubled spirit that disturbs it. I am a good Christian and a poor man, and am not to be daunted by the Devil himself, even though he should come in the shape of a big bag of money!" The mason knew about the money and manipulated the landlord to believe he was just trying to do something good. The mason had been at the house before to help the old priest and knew that there was so much money hidden away. The mason twisted the truth to get what he wanted.

Another criterion of being dishonest is it must be intentional, done knowingly; know that what you're doing is wrong. "The offer of the honest mason was gladly accepted; he moved with his family into the house, and fulfilled all his engagements." The landlord had no idea about the hidden money, and the mason did. The mason didn't say anything and just decided that he would take the house from him. The landlord did not ask, but the mason should have told him about the hidden money because it was the landlord's property. The mason twisted the truth in why he wanted the house to get what he truly wanted, which was the money.

An existing possibility to find the rightful owner or the truth is the third criteria of being a dishonest person. If the mason would have came clean at the beginning by saying that he knew there was money in the house that the landlord can use then he would not be a dishonest man. Instead the mason decided to keep the information to himself to benefit his own needs. There was a definite possibility for the truth to be brought out, but the mason decided to not let anyone know. He did not even let his family know until he was on his death bed.

The last criteria that the mason met to be a dishonest man is the intention to deceive, cheat, or deprive someone of something rightfully his or hers. Even though the priest had died and did not leave his money to anyone, it was not the mason's money to have. Instead it should have gone to the landlord since it was his property. The mason deprived the landlord of what was rightfully his which makes him a dishonest man.

The mason was a dishonest man by accomplishing all the criteria of being untruthful. He lied to the landlord about what was really hidden in the house just to benefit himself. Being a dishonest person can be a very bad thing in life and may come back to haunt you.

Stage 5. Individual Application of Procedures

The students move beyond the earlier scaffolds and apply the procedures they have learned to create their own extended definition of a concept.

EPISODE 5.1 Begin by having students brainstorm concepts they can focus on. Possibilities include *friendship, maturity, leadership, loyalty* (or *misguided* or *misplaced loyalty*), *integrity, patriotism, responsibility, terrorism, progress, cruelty to animals, maturity, success, sportsmanship,* what *freedom of speech* allows in a school setting, what *equal opportunity* means in a school setting, and so forth.

EPISODE 5.2 Ask each student to select a concept to define and then write his or her own set of scenarios (similar to the ones in Figure 7–2) related to that concept. Then have students use the scenarios to create a set of defining criteria (like those for the Carnegie Hero Award or for dishonesty). Groups of students working on the same concept can share their ideas.

EPISODE 5.3 Have students draft their compositions. They can draw from the scenarios they have created for examples and contrasting examples for each criterion or think of additional or different examples to include. As you monitor students' progress, you might use writing that students have produced earlier in the unit as models for how to incorporate the parts of an extended definition—criteria, examples, contrasting examples, and warrants.

EPISODE 5.4 Have students, in groups of three, read one another's work and suggest revisions based on these questions:

1. Does the composition have an introduction that catches the reader's interest and presents the concept that will be defined? How does it establish the need for or importance of a definition of the concept?

2. Does the introduction present a set of criteria for defining the concept? What are the criteria presented?

3. For each criterion presented in the introduction, what example and contrasting example does the writer provide to clarify the criterion?

4. Which criteria and/or examples are difficult to understand or confusing? Explain.

5. What ways can you suggest to improve any of the criteria or examples and contrasting examples?

6. Has the writer employed a warrant to explain how each example and contrasting example does or does not illustrate the criterion? If warrants are missing or unconvincing, how could the writer provide or improve them?

7. How does the writer conclude the composition?

8. What part of the composition is clearest or best explained? Why?

9. What suggestions can you make for the writer?

Have the students work on a final draft of their essay, either in class or on their own (your call, based on how much support you think they need). Evaluate the essays in terms of the qualities you have discussed and elaborated on in class: introduction of the concept; definition of the concept in terms of criteria, examples, contrasting examples, and warrants; and a conclusion discussing what the term means for human conduct. Whether the language and mechanics exhibited in the essay communicate ideas clearly and appropriately could also be addressed.

EPISODE 5.5

Extensions

1. An extended definition essay rarely appears on a state, district, or college-entrance writing test. However, writing assessments that include elements of argument or persuasion often call for an extended definition (though it is rarely stated as such). For example, an assessment prompt might ask students to select a hero of the year and persuade others that this person deserves the award. In writing the composition, students will need to base their arguments on a definition of a hero or a hero of the year and then argue how the person they have selected fulfills the criteria. Have students practice writing for an assessment by using this prompt or another that

requires an argument based on a definition. Practice with topics like this will help students identify when an extended definition is needed in writing for various purposes and audiences.

2. Include an extended definition composition in a conceptual unit (see Smagorinsky 2008 and www.coe.uga.edu/~smago/VirtualLibrary/Unit_Outlines.htm). Many conceptual units are based on an extended definition of a concept—the hero (or the mythic hero, or the epic hero, or the tragic hero), coming of age (maturity versus immaturity), courageous action, a good female role model (see Johannessen, Kahn, and Walter 2009), a good parent (see Kahn et al. 1984), romantic love, the American Dream, and so forth. An ongoing element of these units is arriving at an extended definition of the focus concept.

What Makes This Sequence a Structured Process Approach?

The design and sequence of the activities in this chapter are based on instructional scaffolding. The setting moves from whole-class and teacher-led instruction to small-group practice to whole-class sharing of small-group work to individual performance. Each setting provides different degrees of support and feedback as students work out the procedures they will use to produce extended definitions. Assessment emphasizes students' application of procedures to new problems rather than how well they have memorized information provided by teachers and texts.

As the teacher, you will have worked outside class to locate and/or prepare the materials students analyze and discuss in class (the Carnegie Hero Award documents, for example). The instruction is broken down into manageable segments so that students focus on one feature of extended definition at a time. Yet because each feature is meaningless without the others, students' thinking is always integrated.

The emphasis is on procedures for how to think and write about extended definitions. The topics are accessible, involving established materials (the Carnegie Hero Award), a story without a definition (the "honest mason" activity), and topics of students' choosing (when they apply the procedures for extended definition to a concept they know about and are interested in). Rather than starting off with an extended definition of Transcendentalism or Existentialism, the students begin with relatively familiar and accessible content, which enables them to focus on the definition and its components without having to learn large amounts of challenging new content at the same time.

Because the instruction has centered on procedures, not final form, after completing the sequence students will know how to go about defining abstract terms in the future. Structured process instruction goes beyond the next exam and serves students well in dealing with similar problems encountered later.

Questions for Reflection

1. What current events in the nation or local community involve or focus on the definition of a concept? How could one or more specific current events or situations be used to "hook" student interest in writing extended definition essays?

2. The Carnegie Hero Award provides a set of defining criteria that can serve as a model for students. What other possible sources of "real world" criteria could also serve as models?

3. Choose a concept that is the focus of a unit in middle or high school English language arts, such as coming of age (maturity versus immaturity) or the American Dream. How might you develop a set of scenarios (such as those for dishonesty in Figure 7–2) that would help students develop an extended definition of the key concept? What kinds of situations would you include? What criteria would they lead to?

4. What are some novels, short stories, and/or poems (such as "The Adventure of the Mason") that involve the definition of a concept as central to their meaning? How might such works be used in teaching extended definition writing?

5. This chapter includes a minilesson on introducing warrants using phrases and clauses. What other difficulties do you anticipate that students might have in terms of language usage and conventions when writing a definition essay? What additional minilessons might you develop?

6. How could technology be incorporated in helping students learn to write definition essays?

7. How could blogs, wikis, or other interactive technology be used in helping students as they learn to write definition essays?

8. What particular difficulties do you anticipate that ELL students or struggling readers will have with writing extended definition essays? What activities would you develop or what adjustments would you make to assist them?

9. What activities would you develop to help students reflect on the thinking and writing processes they used in creating an extended definition essay?

10. When you are commenting on students' extended definition essays, what kinds of comments do you think will be most helpful to students? What kinds of comments would be least helpful? What specific comments and/or suggestions would you make for Jessica, who wrote "A Dishonest Man"?

Teaching Research Papers

M ost English/language arts curricula include a formal research paper at some point in middle and/or high school. While a few include some form of original research in which students design their own study or survey and gather their own data, most ask students to gather information from books, articles, Internet sources, and so forth and incorporate this material into a report that includes formal citations: works cited, references, or a bibliography.

Most teachers, parents, and students consider the ability to comprehend, analyze, and synthesize facts, ideas, and concepts from a variety of sources—and to use proper forms of documentation—to be essential in future formal education and in life. Larson (1988) even argues that writing the "junior theme" is an important bonding experience, a shared rite of passage. While writing a term paper, Larson found, students experience "a range of emotional states that are well out of their normal school experience. Many go through a process of personal involvement and self-searching that resembles an identity quest. As a result of the project students feel they have acquired a new status, one that separates them from the uninitiated and puts them closer to the status and power of an autonomous adult" (267).

Unfortunately, students often find it very difficult to analyze and synthesize material. They frequently end up pasting together a string of ideas into a composition that lacks focus and coherence and says little that is meaningful, insightful, or even comprehensible. Some educators suggest that the problem with research papers is that students write on remote or uninteresting topics and that better topic selection will produce better papers (Lamm 1998, among many other sources). Undoubtedly, writing on the assigned topic of how the skin color of sixteenth-century North African Muslims informs one's reading of *Othello, the Moor of Venice* might not inspire a student whose primary interest in life is repairing car engines. But simply providing ten thousand topics for research papers, as Lamm has done, is hardly a solution.

One way to help students avoid disengaged and uninspired research reporting is to have them focus on argumentation related to a topic they're interested in and include some original research in addition to gathering information from sources. This way, their inquiry advances their ability to persuade others of their beliefs, and they have a reason to seek additional information to support their views.

Task Analysis

The basic procedures involved in argument, derived from Toulmin (1957) and Toulmin et al. (1984), are presented in Chapter 5. In writing an argumentation research paper, students need to:

- Take a position on an issue, stated as a *thesis*.

- Support *claims* with specific *data* or *evidence*.

- Include *warrants* to clarify the connection between the data (evidence) and the claim.

- Anticipate *counterarguments* or *counterevidence*.

- Respond to or *rebut* counterarguments or counterevidence.

They also need to know how to format bibliographical citations.

Your instruction begins with an activity based on an accessible topic that students have strong opinions about. (This way, research skills don't have to be taught at the outset.) The topic should also be controversial (i.e., it is *debatable* or *raises doubts*), so students, while arguing a thesis by means of claims, evidence, and warrants, can evaluate and respond to opposing claims and have their own thinking critiqued by others.

After this initial discussion, students learn the formal language of argumentation to apply to the ideas they have already generated.

The argumentative thrust continues as students move from spoken argument to online, real-time written exchanges on an Internet "chat" site. Students spontaneously exchange opinions, claims, evidence, and warrants, rebutting one another's claims in the (anticipated) event of disagreement. Rather than introducing Toulmin's terminology at the outset, instruction again relies on first generating ideas, and only later identifying the components of argument as students examine how they have stated, illustrated, warranted, and defended their beliefs.

Next, students gather information as a way to strengthen their arguments. The role of research is thus to help students argue more effectively with their peers about topics they care about.

Instruction in writing research reports often focuses on aspects of form: how to write a bibliographic entry according to the style guide of the Modern Language Association (MLA) or other standard form, how to produce a note card (even long after computers have provided alternatives), and so on. Teachers may also show students how to find a trustworthy source on the Internet, locate sources in encyclopedias and other print media, and otherwise locate information.

Translating this information into a coherent report or argument gets less attention. As a result, students are always concerned about the fine line between reporting information found in a source and plagiarizing; knowing how to assemble the information they have gathered into a properly documented presentation in their own voice has baffled students for generations. However, when the thrust of the writing shifts from the information as an end in itself to the advancement of an opinion based on that information, plagiarizing becomes less of an issue: students concentrate on fashioning the information into evidence.

In the lesson sequence that follows, students discuss controversial issues, use argumentation to present a more credible and persuasive perspective, and receive continual feedback on their thinking and writing. Students learn procedures by participating in activities and develop criteria for assessment as they generate their ideas.

Stage 1. Gateway Activity: What Makes a Strong Argument?

Begin by debating a student on an inherently interesting and controversial topic: which team has the best chance of winning an upcoming local or national sports event, whether the school should ban MP3 players or cell

EPISODE 1.1

phones, whether lunch periods in the cafeteria should be accompanied by music played by student DJs, whether students should be allowed off campus during the school day. Select an outgoing, vocal student, and work out your respective positions before class (the rest of the students don't have to know that the argument has been staged, if not scripted). As an alternative, ask another teacher, or an administrator, to debate you.

EPISODE 1.2 Ask students to discuss what arguments were raised, which were strongest/ weakest, and why. Ask them to identify what evidence, if any, was provided to support each person's claims. Your goal is to prompt students to develop criteria for what makes an argument effective and convincing. As students identify most of the relevant features, suggest some common terminology (e.g., claim, evidence, warrants, counterarguments).

Then tell students that these are the elements they will focus on as they write a research paper supporting their position on an issue of their choice. As an example, you might take one claim from the previous discussion and explicate it, labeling each feature:

Overall thesis: Students should not be allowed to have cell phones in the school building or on the school grounds.

Claim 1: Students are too undisciplined with their phones, and if they are allowed to have them at school, they will spend too much time calling, texting, searching the Internet, downloading and playing games, and doing other things that distract them from their academic work.

Evidence: In the span of one week, a student used his cell phone to photograph other students relieving themselves in the washroom and posted the photos on the Internet; another used her cell phone camera to photograph quiz questions early in the day and send them to her friends to help them prepare for their quiz in a later period; another used the Internet function to get test answers while taking the exam; and a student arranged a drug deal in a school washroom by making calls on his cell phone.

Warrant: Even though cell phones may be used for legitimate purposes, such as contacting parents or maintaining contact with the outside world during school emergencies, they are too often used for unethical purposes; therefore the overall effect of allowing cell phones in school is deleterious to students' academic attention and their moral conduct in school.

You might also look at counterarguments or counterevidence students have presented and consider how they could be responded to and rebutted. In addition to argumentation, then, a research paper may incorporate elements of other types of writing tasks that we cover in other chapters, such as definition and comparison/contrast.

Stage 2. Researching an Issue

Introduce an issue currently in the news, such as the role of schools in making sure that students eat healthy foods. Should middle and high schools sell junk food in the cafeteria, in vending machines, and at athletic events on school property? Should all junk food be eliminated from middle and high schools? Explain to students that together you will focus on this issue in the context of learning how to write a research paper.

EPISODE 2.1

Spend some time defining and illustrating types of "unhealthy food" or "junk food" found in many schools. For example:

- Free and reduced-price breakfasts that feature pancakes made with white flour, sugar, and salt and served with oleomargarine and sugar-based syrup, and breakfast cereals made from processed flour that are high in sugar and calories.

- Vending-machine potato chips, corn chips, candy bars, sugary soft drinks, and similar products.

- Cheeseburgers, french fries, slices of cake and pie, sugar-based beverages, canned string beans that have been cooked into limp strands of vitamin-depleted mush, and other unhealthy food.

Shops near schools also feature ice cream, fast food, unhealthy snacks, and similar fare.

This discussion needn't be as involved as the definition activities in Chapter 7, but it should at least try to distinguish what is and what is not junk food. For example, you could identify all the food available in the school and classify it as junk food or not, the criteria for a definition emerging as the students compare and contrast the various products. Another option is to begin with a formal definition of junk food from an authoritative source.

Alternatively, you could have students grapple with the junk food problem in small groups (which allows a higher rate of participation) and follow it with a whole-class discussion. In the best of all possible worlds, having students generate definitions inductively in small groups allows them to own their definitions and classifications, but this more time-consuming approach might not fit your schedule.

You could also ask students to research the food served in the school's cafeteria and vending machines:

- Find out what food is available.

- Categorize the food available as either junk food or healthy food.

- Observe five different (unnamed) students during lunch, list what each student is eating, and categorize each item as junk food or healthy food.

Ask students to bring their notes to class, and then have them compile the results.

EPISODE 2.2   Hand out information similar to that in the examples below about junk food in school and ask the students to read it. Alternatively, either on your own or with the students' help, gather several articles for them to read containing credible information on the issue. Then have your students, in small groups, use a chart similar to the one in Figure 8–1 to summarize the arguments and evidence that can be or have been raised on both sides of the issue. Finally, have students, as a class, share the information on their charts.

Information About Junk Food in Schools

Aptos Middle School

Beginning in January 2003, Aptos Middle School, in the San Francisco Unified School District, replaced junk food in the cafeteria with healthy choices. Soda, chips, mega-colossal burgers (58 percent fat), chicken wings (61 percent fat), and hot dogs (77 percent fat) were eliminated.

Students were surveyed about their favorite healthy choices, and based on the results, items such as sushi, deli sandwiches, baked chicken with rice, freshly made soup, salads, and fruit desserts were added. All drinks with added sugar were removed, including those in vending machines. Only 100 percent fruit juices, water, and milk are now available.

Dana Woldow, chair of the Aptos PTSA Student Nutrition Committee explained, "We tried to make sure that every choice we offered contained nutrients, not just empty calories. . . . It is not enough that our food be less bad for the kids. We want the food to be good for them. Our turkey and roast beef sandwiches are made with lots of fresh lettuce and tomato. The homemade soups are loaded with vegetables."

Converting to healthy food choices has increased the profits of Aptos' food service from losing money in 2002 to finishing 2003 more than $6,000 in the black. Aptos (860 students) made more than $2,000 in May 2003, while A.P. Giannini (1,280 students), which still sells soda and junk food, made less than $90 for the month.

Teachers and administrators report that eliminating junk food significantly improved student behavior after lunch and reduced litter. Parents feel less pressure to pack their kids' lunches every day because they know their children will not be tempted to spend their lunch money on poor food choices.

> "Junk Food Out, Profits In at San Francisco Middle School," July 13, 2003, website of Parents Advocating School Accountability, San Francisco (www.pasasf.org).

Childhood Obesity

1976–1980: 6.5% of 6–11-year-olds and 5.0% of 12–19-year-olds are overweight

1988–1994: 11.3% of 6–11-year-olds and 10.5% of 12–19-year-olds are overweight

1999–2000: 15.1% of 6–11-year-olds and 14.8% of 12–19-year-olds are overweight

2003–2004: 18.8% of 6–11-year-olds and 17.4% of 12–19-year-olds are overweight

> From the National Health and Nutrition Examination Survey conducted by the Centers for Disease Control and Prevention. Source: National Center for Health Statistics. Found in "Update: Junk Food in Schools," March 23, 2007, *Issues & Controversies On File*, Facts On File News Services, www.2facts.com.

Vending Machines

Vending machines with junk food are a significant source of money for many schools, generating more than $750 million each year. In 2000, High Point High School made nearly $100,000 from vending machines in the school. That amount was about 25% of the school's operating budget. William Ryan, principal of High Point High School, in Prince George's County, Maryland, says, "This money is crucial. There are things that I do with that money around the school for the students that I could not do [without it]."

Figure 8–1. Should Middle Schools and High Schools Eliminate Junk Food Sales in the Cafeteria, in Vending Machines, and at Athletic Events?

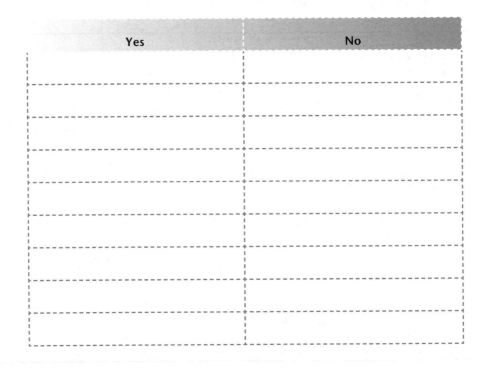

Yes	No

With tight budgets and decreasing money from the government, schools often have to cut music, athletic, and art programs, as well as technology and library resources.

From "Junk Food in Schools," January 24, 2007, *Issues & Controversies On File,* Facts On File News Services, www.2facts.com.

Berkeley, California, Public Schools

A well-respected chef, Ann Cooper, was brought in to make changes in the cafeterias of 16 of Berkeley's public schools. She introduced whole-wheat veggie pizza with toppings like zucchini, blue cheese, and walnuts, but trash cans were filled with uneaten slices. More than 200 students signed a petition protesting the pizza and other new offerings. In her first year, Cooper went tens of thousands of dollars over budget and lost many students as customers.

From "Slow Food Movement," by Sarah Glazer, in *CQ Researcher,* Volume 17, January 26, 2007, pages 73–96, http://library.cqpress .com/cqresearcher/cqresrre2007012600

Naperville, Illinois, Middle and High Schools

Schools in Naperville District 203 resemble health clubs, with heart monitors, treadmills, stair-steppers, and even a rock-climbing wall. According to Phil Lawler, physical education coordinator, "instead of teaching sports skills," gym classes focus on "health, wellness and lifestyle. So many are pointing the finger at poor nutrition, but a bigger factor is kids are just not physically active. Physical education for every kid in school could be the solution to get control of health care." While running laps, students are scored on their performances within their own heart zones, not on how well they compete against others. Student cholesterol tests have improved every year since testing began in 1994. Fitness tests also show gains, with only 3 percent of Naperville ninth-graders considered overweight.

From "The Shape We're In: Innovative Schools Teach Lifelong Health by Just Saying No to Status Quo," by Lorna Collier, *Philadelphia Inquirer*, May 27, 2003, SIRS Knowledge Source, http://sks.sirs.com.

EPISODE 2.3

By now, students may realize that their arguments do not have the support needed to be persuasive. Give them the opportunity to research the additional information they need to develop and defend their positions. You might reserve time in the school library for them to research the issue of junk food and the role of school as an educational institution, using both printed material and Internet sources. Remind students to document these sources so they can include them in their bibliography or list of references.

EPISODE 2.4

If the technology is available, have students blog or "chat" (on blogger.com, for example) about whether schools should eliminate junk food. Remind them to provide evidence for their claims and counterarguments. You can participate as well until students get the idea. For example, if Sam writes, "Students will simply stop eating the cafeteria food, and the school will lose money if no one buys lunches," you might respond, "Interesting point, Sam. Will they not eat anything at all in protest, or will they get food somewhere else?" Or if LaShae says, "It would help students who are overweight," you might respond, "LaShae, you say that eliminating junk food in the cafeteria would help students not be overweight. Can you explain more about why you think it would have this effect?" or, "LaShae, what about students who are in good physical shape and healthy? Is it fair to keep them from having junk food when they want it?" Your goal is to encourage students to elaborate on their thinking and defend their claims. Your comments are also models of how they can respond to their classmates' comments.

After the blogging session, reproduce or project transcripts of the exchanges, and ask students to identify strong arguments and evidence and effective points.

If your classroom is not equipped with computers, substitute a conventional classroom discussion. Although students' oral remarks are more ephemeral and harder to classify than their written comments, an oral exchange is similar and can be the basis of the following classification activity.

EPISODE 2.5

Take aspects of one of the previous arguments and label them clearly so that students understand what they need to accomplish when making a point. Here's an example:

Overall thesis: Junk food should not be available anywhere in the school because it contributes to the obesity and poor health of students and makes school a site for learning unhealthy habits.

Claim 1: Vending machines, while popular with students and a source of income for the school, primarily serve food products that are high in sugar, salt, fat, chemicals, and other unhealthy ingredients.

Evidence: For example, the beef jerky sold in all the school vending machines includes the following ingredients: beef parts, mechanically separated chicken parts, water, salt, corn syrup, flavorings, dextrose, spices, hydrolyzed corn gluten, soy and wheat gluten proteins, sodium nitrite, and lactic acid starter culture.

Warrant: These ingredients, which are typical of the processed foods found in vending machines, contribute to bad health. There are two sources of salt (table salt and sodium nitrite), which often elevates blood pressure; and two sources of sugar (corn syrup and dextrose), which makes people obese and can make students hyperactive. Hydrolyzed corn gluten is a source of monosodium glutamate (MSG), which in addition to providing yet more sodium, has been found in some studies to cause retinal degeneration and kill brain cells and may lead to behavior disorders, learning disabilities, reproductive disorders, obesity, irritable bowel syndrome, heart irregularities, asthma, and migraine headaches. Lactic acid starter culture is often based on milk and so is dangerous for sufferers of particular allergies.

Counterargument and Rebuttal: Although there might be some beneficial protein in the beef and chicken parts of indeterminate origin, and although there are more of these ingredients than any other individual ingredient, on the whole this food, like other vending machine snacks, is detrimental to one's health and should be avoided. Simply including protein is not a good reason to sell a product if the protein source (especially beef) is implicated in heart disease. Producing beef also contributes to global warming by displacing vegetable farms with beef farms and their cows, who consume additional vegetables that people might eat and produce flatulence that adds climate-warming methane gas to the atmosphere; beef farms are one of the world's greatest threats to climate stability.

Review this argument and emphasize that each claim needs to be clearly related to the main argumentative point and buttressed with evidence and explained in terms of a warrant. When juxtaposed with an argument that supports the availability of junk food in the school, the strengths and weaknesses of the competing arguments can be evaluated relative to one another.

Stage 3. Practicing Warrants

Students who have been taught to write primarily via five-paragraph themes may have little experience relating claims and evidence by means of warrants. Most instruction in expository writing focuses on generalization and support, terms that correspond to claims and evidence. But as Hillocks (2002) observes, the evidence produced in such a template may or may not make sense relative to the claim.

Students will produce stronger evidence for their claims and drive home their points more forcefully when they explain why the evidence supports their claims. Therefore, have them complete the exercise in Figure 8–2, in which they create warrants for given claims and evidence. If students are working with this element of argumentation for the first time, have them do the problems in pairs rather than individually.

Stage 4. Drafting an Essay

At this point students are ready to begin planning their research paper on whether middle and high schools (or their own school in particular) should eliminate junk food from the cafeteria and vending machines.

Have students, in small groups, use a graphic organizer like those provided in Figures 8–3 and 8–4 to remind themselves of the features of an effective argument, organize their material, and get a sense of the best order in which to present their claims. Because students have already discussed the issue at length, they will have a great deal of information to draw on as they discuss their positions and assemble their evidence.

EPISODE 4.1

Figure 8–2. Writing Warrants

Each of the following problems states a claim and then offers evidence to support it. For each pair of statements, provide a warrant that clearly explains why the evidence supports the claim. The claim is stated so that you may take either a pro (for) or con (against) position. Decide which position the evidence supports and, through your warrant, explain why.

Example:

Claim: Soft drinks are [are not] unhealthy because they contain a super-abundance of sugar.

Evidence: One popular cola beverage is made according to the following recipe: 30 cups of sugar, 2 gallons of water, 1 quart of lime juice, 4 ounces of citrate of caffeine, 2 fluid ounces of citric acid, 1 ounce of extract of vanilla, 3/4 fluid ounce of extract of cola, and 3/4 fluid ounce of fluid extract of coca.

Warrant: Because there are 128 ounces of fluid in a gallon, there are 30 cups of sugar per each 256 ounces of water. Adding the remainder of the fluids produces a ratio of 30 cups of sugar in each 296.5 total ounces of fluid, or roughly 1 cup per each 10 ounces of total fluid. Therefore every 12-ounce can of this product includes roughly 1.2 cups of sugar. Because the amount of sugar in each can of the "regular" variety of this beverage is so thoroughly saturated with sugar, this product is likely to contribute to its consumer's obesity.

Either by yourself or with a partner, provide a warrant relating each of the following claims to the supporting evidence:

1. *Claim*: Potato chips are [are not] unhealthy because the way in which they are prepared is [is not] unhealthy for the human body.

    Evidence: Potato chips are made by slicing each potato into a thin oval and deep-frying it in vegetable oil, then adding salt and additional flavors.

    Warrant:

2. *Claim*: The pancakes served in the free and reduced-price breakfast program are [are not] detrimental to one's health.

    Evidence: The pancakes are made from processed flour, sugar, salt, eggs, and baking soda, and are served with butter and cane syrup.

    Warrant:

(continues)

Figure 8–2. Writing Warrants *(continued)*

3. *Claim*: The sausages served in the free and reduced-price breakfast program should [should not] be considered junk food.

   Evidence: Inexpensive sausages of the sort served in these breakfasts contain up to 50% fat and have a salt content of 2–3%. They are additionally cured with salt and sodium nitrite, making them very salty. The meat itself comes from every part of the pig, meaning that a sausage may include bone remnants, intestines, internal organs, ground hooves, and other parts that few people would eat by choice.

   Warrant:

4. *Claim*: Removing junk food in vending machines will [will not] significantly reduce funds for important school programs.

   Evidence: According to one principal, her school now receives nearly $100,000 a year from vending machines. That money is used to pay for girls' and boys' volleyball teams, boys' and girls' cross country track teams, and girls' and boys' gymnastics teams.

   Warrant:

5. *Claim*: When healthy choices are available along with junk food, students will [will not] tend to select the healthy options.

   Evidence: On a typical day at River Grove High School, the lunch featured grilled chicken breasts, rice, steamed broccoli, and a fruit cup of fresh watermelon cubes. The cafeteria reported that 819 out of 1,120 students purchased this lunch selection, while the rest selected less healthy options.

   Warrant:

6. *Claim*: The ingredients in candy bars are [are not] unhealthy and make [do not make] it hard for students to concentrate and sit still during class.

   Evidence: One popular candy bar is made from water, corn syrup, butter, vanilla extract, peanut butter, salt, sugar, caramel, peanuts, and chocolate chips.

   Warrant:

(continues)

Figure 8–2. Writing Warrants *(continued)*

7. *Claim*: Pizza slices should not [should] be served in school because they have little [great] nutritional value.

   Evidence: The typical plain pizza slice has 272 calories, 88 of which come from fat. Nearly half of the calories come from carbohydrates, which convert to sugar as part of digestion. The fat content amounts to 9.8 grams, 4.4 of which are saturated. A pizza slice includes 22 mg of cholesterol and 551 mg of sodium, along with 4.1 grams of sugar and 33 grams of carbohydrates. These figures are greatly increased when pepperoni, extra cheese, sausage, and other unhealthy toppings are added.

   Warrant:

8. *Claim*: Fruit juices should [should not] be sold in schools if they contain ingredients other than fruit juice.

   Evidence: Most fruit juices sold contain such ingredients as water, high fructose corn syrup, citric acid, ascorbic acid, dyes that produce an artificial color, "other ingredients," and 5% fruit juice.

   Warrant:

9. *Claim*: Pork rinds are [are not] very unhealthy and should not [should] be sold in schools.

   Evidence: Pork rinds are typically made from pork skins, pork rinds, salt, lactose, sodium diacetate, salt, malic acid, modified food starch, corn syrup solids, acetic acid, soybean oil, citric acid, sodium citrate, chili peppers, paprika, and monosodium glutamate. For each serving of 1/2 ounce, the consumer ingests 80 calories (45 from fat), 5 grams of fat (2 grams are saturated), 15 mg of cholesterol, and 960 mg of sodium.

   Warrant:

10. *Claim*: Focusing gym classes on physical fitness and good health is [is not] a better solution than eliminating all junk food from schools.

   Evidence: A school district in Naperville, Illinois, that focused gym classes on teaching students physical fitness, health, and wellness instead of sports skills found that only three percent of its ninth graders were overweight.

   Warrant:

Figure 8–3. Graphic Organizer 1

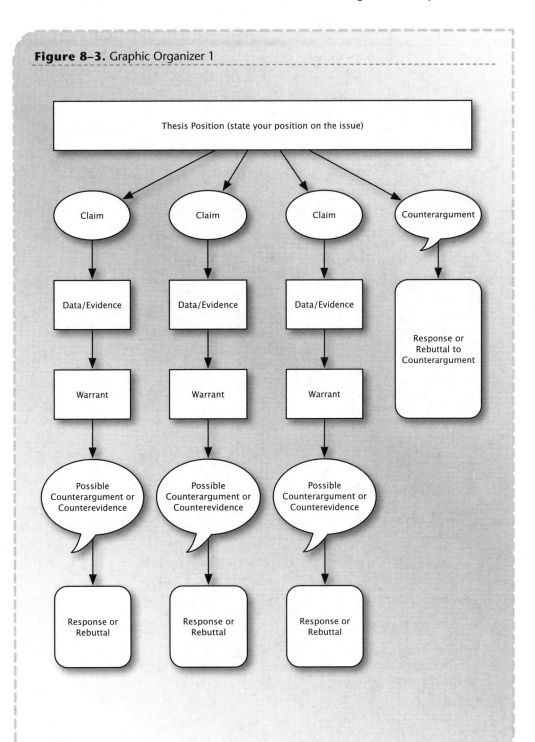

Figure 8–4. Graphic Organizer 2

Overall Thesis:

Claim #1

Evidence

Warrant

Claim #2

Evidence

Warrant

Claim #3

Evidence

Warrant

Claim #4

Evidence

Warrant

Claim #5

Evidence

Warrant

Claim #6

Evidence

Warrant

Counterargument or Counterevidence

Response or Rebuttal

Other Counterargument or Counterevidence

Response or Rebuttal

Conclusion

Figure 8–5. Guiding Questions for Evaluating an Argumentation Research Paper

Is the author's overall thesis stated and fleshed out clearly and consistently in the introductory paragraph?

Is the paper organized so that the argument comes across as a series of related claims?

Is each claim clearly related to the overall thesis statement?

Is each claim supported by convincing evidence?

Is the evidence tied to the claim by means of a warrant?

Is a counterargument or counterevidence stated and rebutted?

Is there a concluding paragraph that sums up the author's position and that reinforces the overall thesis statement?

Does the paper make sense as a whole, or do some parts veer away from the overall thesis statement?

Using the guiding questions in Figure 8–5, ask your students to help you create a rubric for evaluating their writing. Correlate your specific expectations with their critiques of one another's ideas and writing to this point. The degree to which they must satisfy each requirement depends on their age, their prior experience with this sort of writing, and other factors.

EPISODE 4.2

Have students write the first draft of their essay. Based on the realities of your classroom and your students' response to your instruction up to this point, decide whether to have them do this in class or as homework and how much time to give them.

EPISODE 4.3

Stage 5. Peer-Group Response and Author Revision

Have students, in small groups, use the guiding questions in Figure 8–5 to evaluate one another's essays and give and receive feedback on the quality and persuasiveness of their positions. One purpose of this small-group critique is to point out areas in which the evidence is not sufficient to support a claim and suggest additional sources of evidence. Research thus becomes a tool for arguing convincingly rather than a task to be completed in isolation.

EPISODE 5.1

EPISODE 5.2   Ask students to revise their essay, seeking new sources of information to support their claims if necessary.

EPISODE 5.3   Have students, in small groups, once again use the guiding questions in Figure 8–5 to critique one another's work. Give them time to make final revisions.

Stage 6. Attending to Bibliographic Form

Because students have organized their essays as a series of claims supported by evidence and explained by warrants, their final drafts, for the most part, will consist of a logical sequence of information with appropriate paragraphing. Now it's time to consider how to present citations.

There are a number of options, depending on the discipline. The MLA guidelines (Gibaldi 2003) employed in university English departments and taught by many high school English teachers are customarily used in the humanities. But the social sciences—education, psychology, and other fields that study people rather than texts—follow the recommendations codified in the *Publication Manual of the American Psychological Association* (2001). The *Chicago Manual of Style* (the fifteenth edition was published in 2003), which we followed in writing our own doctoral dissertations, sets out yet another set of rules. And there are countless other grammar and composition textbooks. Rather than learning *the* style for formatting research papers, students are learning *a* style.

Your final task is to choose an appropriate format and help students understand the conventions you expect. Online sources are a convenient way to let students see the appropriate order in which to list the segments of their citations. Numerous online sources can be found by searching "MLA Citation Style," "APA Citation Style," and so forth, using Google or another search engine. That accomplished, students hand in their essays for your evaluation.

Extensions

1. Have students conduct research related to the literature of historical periods (Victorian, Elizabethan, American Transcendentalist, and so on). How did Thoreau represent a Transcendentalist perspective? Was Richard Wright a Realist or a Naturalist? How accurate is Shakespeare's portrayal of thirteenth-century society in Verona and Mantua in *Romeo and Juliet*?

2. Let students experiment with other ways of presenting research. They could produce a documentary film on the hazards of eating junk food, create a website that sorts through the critical issues in their topic of interest, develop a work of drama or fiction conveying their perspective on an issue, contribute to web-based listservs and bulletin boards, or speak in public forums.

What Makes This Sequence a Structured Process Approach?

The instruction described in this chapter scaffolds students' learning as they first argue based on what they already know and then extend that knowledge through research. Your out-of-class preparation includes creating lists of possible topics; identifying Internet chat rooms and message boards; and preparing graphic organizers, a rubric, and a warranting exercise. The research is conducted in a highly social and often collaborative manner; students help one another develop argumentation strategies and locate appropriate evidence to support their claims.

The writing students do helps them become more articulate and persuasive in making their points. It also helps them respond to opposing perspectives critically yet openly; a student might change positions based on the more persuasive arguments of classmates. The instruction is grounded in students' authentic need to "argue to learn": to exchange views as a way to grow intellectually and come to a clearer understanding of who they are and what they believe.

Questions for Reflection

1. What current events or issues in the nation or local community might be used to "hook" student interest in writing research papers?

2. What possible topics that may be of interest to students would be problematic to focus instruction on? What guidelines would you use to determine topics that teachers (or students) should avoid?

3. What topic do you think would be good to use as an alternative to the junk food issue in this chapter? What kinds of sources/information (such as those in Figure 8–1) would you develop for students to examine and analyze?

4. When students are using technology to find evidence, it is important that the sources they find are reliable, valid sources for their purpose. What kinds of activities would you develop to help students learn how to evaluate the validity of sources on the Internet or elsewhere?

5. Beyond the suggestions incorporated in this chapter, in what other ways could technology be incorporated to help students learn to write research papers?

6. What are the characteristics of an effective introduction and conclusion for a research paper? What activities would you develop to help students who are struggling with writing effective introductions and/or conclusions?

7. This chapter includes a mini-lesson on writing warrants. What particular difficulties do you anticipate that students might have in terms of language usage and conventions when writing a research paper? What additional mini-lessons might you develop?

8. What particular difficulties do you anticipate that ELL students or struggling readers will have with writing research papers? What activities would you develop or what adjustments would you make to assist them?

9. What activities would you develop to help students reflect on the thinking and writing processes they used in creating a research paper?

10. When you are commenting on students' final papers, what kinds of comments do you think will be most helpful to students? What kinds of comments would be least helpful? What guidelines would you develop to help teachers focus their comments to be most helpful to students?

PART III

The
Bigger
Picture

9

Putting It All Together
Creating a Writing Curriculum

Writing instruction rarely occurs in isolation. Rather, it is part of a broader curriculum that includes the historic strands of language and literature and, these days, electronic texts, music, film, and other media as well. What might writing instruction encompassing these varied means of expression look like?

First, what do we mean by *curriculum*? The term is rooted in the Latin word for *racecourse*, suggesting that a curriculum is the course of study students pursue on their way to adulthood and a vocation. While some feel that this course should be run competitively, others believe that racing through the curriculum serves students poorly, in the way it pits them against one another, puts a premium on covering ground rapidly, and implies that everyone is headed toward the same finish line.

Many curricula indeed suggest that students' experiences should be uniform in terms of what they learn, when they learn it, where they are headed after graduation, and much else. In some districts every teacher at the same grade level in every school is teaching the same lesson from the same script on the same day. As teachers, we find this approach to be very unstimulating, both for us and for our students.

Our approach to a writing curriculum places far more authority in the hands of teachers, who must always adjust their instruction to their particular classroom. We do not imagine that it will be followed to the letter by every teacher in every class. Rather, we're providing a blueprint of possibilities that teachers might consider as they interpret and implement the curriculum. What follows is undoubtedly idealistic, or at least unencumbered by local demands and restrictions. Any effort to institute this general plan in any particular setting will inevitably require negotiation.

General Principles

A writing curriculum can play out in any number of ways. Most widely adopted grammar and composition textbooks, for instance, assume an ongoing attention to form as the central organizing principle. Students are led through a systematic and comprehensive set of lessons covering the formal rules governing syntax, parts of speech, and word usage. In addition there are lessons covering forms of composition, especially the five-paragraph theme. It is assumed that as a consequence of such study, students will be able to write and speak according to the rules to which they have been exposed. Our interactions with young people (not to mention adults) over the years tell us that this assumption is flawed.

In their review of research on the English/language arts curriculum, Burroughs and Smagorinsky (2009) found that although theories and biases in establishing curriculum abound, there is virtually no research to back them up—no doubt because research is difficult to conduct, given the complexity of trying to determine curricular effects on students while filtering out other influences. As an analogy, consider the research on drinking coffee. Studies have found that people who drink four or more cups of coffee a day greatly increase their chances of dying young. But it turns out that there's more going on than just drinking lots of coffee; coffoholics also tend to smoke more, exercise less, have less healthy diets, and drink more alcohol at the end of the day (to offset the caffeine rush) than do people who drink coffee in moderation. Drinking coffee, then, is difficult to identify as the source of bad health; perhaps it's merely symptomatic of an unhealthy lifestyle.

The effects of a curriculum are similarly confounded by the quality of teaching, the economic level of the community, the way in which a curriculum's effects are measured, the amount of teaching time dedicated to test preparation versus other priorities, class size, the degree of students' affiliation with the institution of school, and much else. Studying the effects of a curriculum on student learning is just too messy and gargantuan a project to do well, so people resort to developing theories of what will happen instead of conducting investigations of what does happen. We are no different from others in taking this relatively easy way out.

We do, however, have a lot of experience in a lot of schools. We've been K–12 students in schools for a collective fifty years or so, albeit long ago. Together we have about 130 years of experience teaching in schools, serving as district administrators, and visiting classrooms as university professors involved in research and teacher education. We've seen all manner of curricula at work and talked with innumerable teachers and students about their experiences. To help us understand these experiences and observations, we've done quite a bit of reading about curriculum theory. We feel that's a sound basis for the principles that guide our thinking about the big picture of K–12 writing instruction.

A Spiral Curriculum

Many educators believe that once something has been taught, it needn't and perhaps shouldn't be taught again. Want proof? Propose that a story taught to ninth graders be taught again to tenth graders. We've done so, to the bewilderment of colleagues who believe that specific pieces of literature should be taught at one and only one grade level.

We disagree with the idea that a single experience with something is definitive. Instead, we embrace Jerome Bruner's (1960) belief that a curriculum should proceed as a spiral rather than a straight line. In other words, because learning benefits from reinforcement and repetition, we need to provide recurring experiences with texts, ideas, and ways of expressing ideas about texts. With each reiteration, students develop new understanding based on what they have learned since their previous experience with the text, idea, or medium of expression.

A spiral curriculum requires that we reconsider conventional scope and sequence charts. These plans usually ensure that at some point during the six, seven, or eight years of middle and high school, each and every skill or competency expected of an articulate adult is covered, and in a particular order that may or may not make sense developmentally. Such outlines of comprehensive language competencies are too immense to be taught effectively in the time allocated; as middle school teacher Natalie Gibson learned, "It would actually take something like twenty-five years to teach [the county's eighth-grade] curriculum!" (Smagorinsky et al. 2004, 242). The notion of a spiral curriculum is less prescriptive and less rigid, while still codifying a course of instruction that benefits student learning.

In a spiral curriculum, students journey through increasingly sophisticated experiences in some of the same vehicles. Revisiting ideas and experiences allows students to engage in narration and argumentation in increasingly sophisticated forms and in relation to more complex ideas as the readings and concepts become more challenging. Writing a coming-of-age narrative in the ninth grade does not conclude our students' experience with this genre. A narrative may later help them relate to a literary theme, and they will use narrative conventions whenever storytelling is called for, in ever more sophisticated ways: during sophomore year in relation to a new theme (e.g., responsibility) or during junior or senior year's literature strand (e.g., sharing a personal experience with ostracism in connection with reading *The Scarlet Letter* or telling a tale about ambition in connection with reading *Macbeth*).

Integration

There ought to be some connective thread that helps students see relations among the various aspects (topics, activities, goals) of their school experiences. Arthur Applebee (1996) has used the metaphor of a *curricular conversation* to describe the ways in which each individual discussion in a classroom should tie into a broader conversation that helps students see connections among the units and lessons in a course of study. This idea is useful in organizing both writing instruction and the broader teaching in which it is embedded.

Achieving this integration is easier said than done (Applebee et al. 2000). Employing a spiral curriculum that revisits ideas and reinforces genres is one way to help tie a curriculum together and enable long-term conversations about its content. It's also important not to isolate either language or writing instruction from other curricular strands, as often happens, particularly with grammar. While some teachers see advantages in having separate reading and writing workshops, we believe students benefit when literature is taught and written about in connection with themes or other organizing principles.

Inevitably, efforts to integrate curriculum favor depth over breadth: a fragmented curriculum allows broader coverage because ideas suggested by one literary work are not explored in relation to those suggested by another. Deeper rather than broader coverage no doubt means that students will not learn about adverbial particles or second-degree dramatic irony or other arcana that often inflate the English/language arts curriculum guides. But few students remember such obscure knowledge after the test (or during it, for that matter). We believe that useful grammar knowledge is important to have, but are concerned that much grammar instruction is taught more for the sake of knowing grammar as a subject than of knowing grammar for clearer communication.

Many Means of Access

The more standardized a curriculum, the fewer variations there are in how a student can interact with the material and respond to it with understanding. If a writing program focuses exclusively on the five-paragraph theme, for example, it benefits those students who are most comfortable with this approach to organizing ideas. But it's very clear from cross-cultural studies that not everyone learns to think in the same way (Cole 1996). Gender, ethnicity, race, social class, religion, neuropsychological makeup, and other cultural factors—not to mention good old individuality—ensure that students have unique strengths and dispositions. If the purpose of educational experience and assessment is fruitful interaction with the curriculum, it makes sense to be open-minded about how students approach and interpret that curriculum (Gallas and Smagorinsky 2002).

This open-minded perspective means varying how we ask students to respond to and interpret ideas and materials (and at times letting them choose how they will do so). Learning argumentation is important but should not be emphasized at the expense of learning how to write strong narratives, parodies, and dramas or express ideas in countless other ways. Writing involves problem solving, and in order for students to develop a repertoire of problem-solving strategies, they need a variety of writing experiences. By widening the range of student expression in the classroom, teachers can give each student opportunities to learn many forms of composition and open the door to academic success for students whose strengths and culturally learned ways are traditionally underappreciated and given little attention.

Emphasis on Learning Processes

If we want students to achieve a challenging learning goal—understand Mark Twain's use of irony, write a satire, define a contested term (e.g., *success*)—we need to teach them how to do so rather than simply give them assignments and show them models of end products. This book illustrates how to teach composing procedures for several types of writing.

Many and Varied Experiences

Students ought to have as wide a variety of writing experiences as possible. Although students do some writing across the curriculum, most school-based writing still takes place in English class. English teachers should therefore plan their instruction with a great range of writing opportunities in mind.

All writing is not the same. While some general strategies are useful regardless of the situation—freewriting for ideas, outlining or webbing ideas, and so on—writing in response to particular tasks calls for specific sorts of processes and thinking. Furthermore, writing in response to a specific task must meet particular expectations, depending on what the composition is designed to accomplish with specific readers. While the processes for composing poems, stories, grocery lists, thank-you notes, editorials, and research papers all have some things in common, the procedures for thinking and composing are not the same for each. The writing curriculum should help students develop a repertoire of problem-finding, problem-solving, and composing strategies. Ideally, students will learn how to solve the immediate problem presented by a specific type of writing and how to apply these same procedures in new situations of a similar type.

Mapping the range of writing that students do across the English/language arts curriculum helps ensure that students learn to write not only narratives and arguments (and their subgenres) but also extended definitions, research reports, comparison and contrast papers, satires, literary criticism, original creative pieces of various kinds, and other formal types of writing. Students should also have opportunities to write informally in journals, response logs, and similar media.

Structured Sequence of Activities

Allowing students to discover procedures on their own, while perhaps liberating for already fluent writers, is an unnecessary impediment to many other students. The writing instruction we advocate uses teacher-designed activities built around the demands of specific tasks.

The teacher's role is to design a sequence of activities that enables students to inductively develop strategies for engaging with particular kinds of problems. To ensure that this inductive work will result in formal knowledge of how to go about the task in the future, a teacher also needs to orchestrate discussions in which students identify and demonstrate their understanding of the procedures they have used throughout the sequence. With a conscious awareness of their learning processes, students are better able to take on new tasks with similar demands.

Context

Effective instruction also pays attention to the context in which it takes place. The term *context* comes from the Latin root *contexere*, meaning *to weave*. A context is thus not a static set of parameters. People, both individually and collectively, not only act within contexts, they also shape them. The following contextual factors, while often seen as fixed and confining, are more permeable than they appear on the surface.

Assessment

Curriculum, standards, and assessments may be mandated by the federal government (e.g., the No Child Left Behind Act), the state, and the district, and these requirements may or may not overlap. These external bodies may require particular types of writing for assessment (the five-paragraph theme, the narrative, and so on), require students to answer multiple-choice questions about language use or writing process, or make other demands. These mandates are necessary (or inevitable) evils of the profession and we need to accommodate them, even if that means detouring from our instruction at times.

However, many teachers compromise their beliefs to the point where they spend all their time preparing their students to take standardized tests, forgoing any attempt at compelling and stimulating instruction. Waving the white flag to this degree is too much of a concession. It is possible to coordinate instruction with the demands of standardized tests, particularly writing tests. In his study of state-mandated writing assessments, Hillocks (2002) identified a variety of approaches, ranging from the least restrictive (Kentucky's portfolio evaluation) to the most tightly scripted (Illinois' strict adherence to the five-paragraph formula, which the state has since replaced with the ACT writing test). Preparing students for writing assessments is therefore not universally the same; teachers identify what the state will assess and determine what is involved in producing writing of the sort required. Because the five-paragraph theme is so frequently employed for assessment purposes, we'll use it to illustrate how to take an often unwelcome external requirement and integrate it into your instruction as smoothly as possible.

Although some applications of the five-paragraph template are downright silly—as a rubric for assessing students' narrative writing, for example (Hillocks 2002)—it can be a useful means of organization *if* the form is secondary and students' ideas are paramount. The solution, then, is to treat the five-paragraph model as one way in which to present various types of exposition or argumentation. (See the idea-driven approach to teaching argumentation presented in Chapter 5.) This approach is much more stimulating than asking students just to slot information into the five-paragraph format (which, Hillocks argues, need not even make sense in order to score well on some state assessments).

As many have noted (see, for example, Bazerman and Paradis 1991), the features of argument that one group finds persuasive are not necessarily effective with another. Convincing argumentation, then, relies on more than form. It relies on understanding the argumentative conventions that are expected and valued among various groups of people. Basketball coaches who argue with referees do not make their case in the same way lawyers present their case to judges. These are but two of the special environments in which knowing the people and conventions involved suggests the form in which an argument may be presented in order to get the desired results.

(In suggesting the need to understand reader expectations, we are not say-ing teachers should encourage their students cynically to abandon their own true voice. Rather, we are saying that addressing a judge as if she were a ref-eree will probably lack appropriate decorum for the setting and work against a client's best interests.)

Task analysis is made easier when the testing agency provides materials that explain what is expected in relation to the scoring rubric. We may not agree with the assumptions behind these posted expectations and criteria (some leave much to be desired—see Hillocks 2002 and Smagorinsky 2010), but they do clarify the task and help us design appropriate instruction. For examples of how to conduct a task analysis that could be adapted to satisfy-ing an external assessment (argumentation and narration are the most com-mon), see the chapters in Part 2.

This approach will make curricular detours for test preparation less dra-matic and more authentic; they are at least partly embedded in the course of instruction and can be tweaked so that students' writing satisfies their needs and interests.

Community

Less explicit in the curriculum but more immediate is the context provided by the local community and its values, experiences, history, culture, and the like. In some cases these values can force concrete adjustments in the curricu-lum; for example, a group of parents in a community we know signed peti-tions demanding that teachers eliminate student journals in their classrooms (this was part of a broader effort to eliminate any sort of introspection among young people that might challenge the dominant religious beliefs of the com-munity; see Smagorinsky 2002 for the text of the petition).

Even when local political activism is less extreme, teachers may consider adjusting their instruction so that it is relevant to local issues. For instance, many communities across the U.S. are attracting waves of new immigrants, which often result in tensions over jobs, increased feelings of nativism, con-flicts about proper public behavior, and other sources of strife and discord. A teacher might develop units of instruction focused on immigration, cliques, peer pressure, conflict with authority, bullying, and other issues that arise as people from different cultures attempt to coexist or fight for what they see as their rights. Writing could consist of narratives about experiences with cultural conflict, arguments over how public facilities should be allocated and treated, comparisons and contrasts of various ways of viewing public institutions, extended definitions of patriotism or other relevant terms, sat-ires of what strikes students as foolish ways of adapting to new conditions, and so forth.

A 7–12 Writing Curriculum

Figure 9–1 is a blueprint for a 7–12 writing/literature curriculum based on conceptual units (see Hillocks et al. 1971 and Smagorinsky 2008). A conceptual unit is a four- to six-week period of forty-five- to sixty-minute classes each day during which students focus on a *theme* (e.g., coming of age), a *genre* (e.g., satire), an *archetype* (e.g., the trickster), a *strategy* (e.g., understanding irony), a *literary period* (e.g., the Victorian Age), a *movement* (e.g., Transcendentalism), a *region* (e.g., authors of Arizona), or an *author* (e.g., the works of Toni Morrison). As of this writing, the website www.coe .uga.edu/~smago/VirtualLibrary/Unit_Outlines.htm, outlines roughly 150 conceptual units, many of them linked to fully elaborated lesson plans.

Figure 9–1 lists eight conceptual units for each academic year, grades 7–12 (grade 11 is dedicated to American literature; grade 12 is a course in the humanities). This blueprint is idealistic; you may need to sacrifice one or more units to time inevitably lost to fire drills, field trips, pep rallies, test preparation, assemblies, bees and birds flying in through the classroom windows, and other realities of school life.

Nor is there a hard-and-fast order in which to teach these units, either within a grade level or across grade levels. The same unit may be taught in different years, varying the materials, the activities, and the type of writing. This is *one* possible way to think about a curriculum; it is a menu from which to choose instruction appropriate for you and your students, not a rigid scope and sequence for all students to experience in the same order. The suggestions are meant to get you thinking about possibilities for what students might study and write about.

A Writing Curriculum for Sophomore Year

For illustrative purposes, we suggest some possibilities for the sorts of writing students might do during each suggested conceptual unit in the tenth-grade curriculum suggested in Figure 9–1. One approach is to have students do one informal type of writing (e.g., keeping a journal or reading log), one formal essay (e.g., arguing for or against a position in relation to the unit concept), and one creative/multimedia project (e.g., a body biography—i.e., a life-sized human outline of a literary character that students fill with interpretive art and written text; see O'Donnell-Allen 2006). You might also have students produce a major synthesis paper at the end of each semester—either a personal reflection such as a portfolio or a formal analysis integrating learning across the units. (Much of the writing can be produced with either pen and paper or a word-processing program using information found either in a library or on the Internet.)

Figure 9–1. Possible Conceptual Units, Grades 7–12

Grade	Unit 1	Unit 2	Unit 3	Unit 4	Unit 5	Unit 6	Unit 7	Unit 8
7	Friends and Enemies	New Kid on the Block	The Outcast	The Trickster	Wilderness Adventures	Animals as Symbols	The Leader	Taking Perspective
8	Gangs, Cliques, and Peer Pressure	Science Fiction	Values Under Stress	Rites of Passage	Allegory	Loss of Innocence	The Journey	Immigration
9	Coming of Age	Adolescent Relationships	Conflict with Authority	The Family	Time Travelers	Parody	Reading Media	Connotation and Imagery
10	Responsibility	Propaganda	Discrimination	Point of View	Coping with Loss	The Epic Hero	Courageous Action	Loyalty
11	The American Dream	The Puritan Ethic	Protest Literature	Self-Reliance	Progress	Success	Realism	The Banality of Evil
12	Technology, Nature, and Society	Social Responsibility	Gender Roles	Satire	Changing Times	Character as Symbol	Terrorist or Freedom Fighter?	A Sense of Place

Responsibility

A unit centering on responsibility might include texts that challenge students to consider what it means to be responsible and where their responsibilities lie in different situations, with questions such as What value systems influence the characters? How strenuously are the value systems being imposed? From where do the characters derive their sense of responsibility? What forces are testing this sense? How do the characters respond to these forces? How is the conflict resolved? What is the author trying to say about value systems and responsibility in particular? Possible texts include Paul Zindel's YAL novel *The Pigman*, Reginald Rose's play *Thunder on Sycamore Street*, and related readings.

- Formal essay: Narrating a situation in which the student writer had to decide which people or set of rules she or he had a responsibility toward.

- Informal writing: Keeping a double-column reading log in response to the course readings and discussions.

- Creative/multimedia project: Dramatizing one of the formal narratives. Small groups of students either select one group member's story or write a composite story based on the narratives of several group members.

Propaganda

This unit focuses on persuasion in which selected and distorted information is used to advance or harm a cause. Focal questions might include What are the characteristics of propaganda? How can we recognize it? What distinguishes propaganda from other forms of persuasion? Students could explore these questions through their reading of works by George Orwell: *Animal Farm, Writers and the Leviathan*, and others.

- Formal essay: Arguing why a particular text does or does not represent a work of propaganda.

- Informal writing: Maintaining a dialogue journal (handwritten or electronic) with another class member in response to class readings and discussions.

- Creative/multimedia project: Producing a multimedia or multigenre text that advances or harms a cause by using selected and distorted information.

Discrimination

In this unit students consider what it means to discriminate and how discrimination affects others.

- Formal essay: Writing a research report on an act or series of acts involving personal, systematic, or institutional discrimination.

- Informal writing: Taking notes, writing drafts, freewriting, drawing, and otherwise thinking through the unit concepts in a writer's notebook.

- Creative/multimedia project: Collaboratively composing a body biography of a literary character who either discriminates or is a victim of discrimination. (See www.coe.uga.edu/~smago/VirtualLibrary/ Activities_that_Promote_Discussion.htm for a rich menu of ideas for creative and multimedia projects.)

Point of View

This unit focuses on who is narrating a story, what this narration does and does not provide readers, and how readers might evaluate the trustworthiness of the narrator.

- Formal essay: Rewriting a narrative from the point of view of a character different from the one who originally told it.

- Informal writing: Noting in a journal one's reactions to various narrators.

- Creative/multimedia project: Dramatizing a scene from a literary work. Each group presents the same scene from the point of view of a different character.

Coping with Loss

This unit helps students consider their own experiences with loss and those of characters from literature.

- Formal essay: Comparing and contrasting various coping strategies used by real and literary characters for losses of varying severity.

- Informal writing: Maintaining a personal journal about loss.

- Creative/multimedia project: Planning a movie version of a work of literature studied in the unit. Issues include casting, direction, soundtrack, promotional posters and trailers, and other aspects of film production.

The Epic Hero

This unit allows students to consider both their own journeys and those of heroes from mythology, film, literature, and other sources.

- Formal essay: Mocking heroic pretensions in a parody of an epic hero story.

- Informal writing: Keeping a "journey journal" about people who may or may not exhibit heroic qualities.

- Creative/multimedia project: Drawing a "life map" that depicts the student's own journey, including heroic elements such as one's birth, initiation experiences, obstacles, fellow travelers, and so on.

Courageous Action

This unit helps students explore the nature of courageous action, a quality prized in many cultures.

- Formal essay: Writing an extended definition of courageous action, illustrated with examples from the texts studied and the student's own knowledge of people and events.

- Informal writing: Freewriting about actions that may or may not involve courageous action. The examples may be student-chosen, taken from history or current events, or provided by the teacher.

- Creative/multimedia project: Producing a presentation illustrating courageous action through images, music, words, dance, performance, and/or other forms of expression.

Loyalty

In this unit students consider issues of loyalty that inevitably surface as their friends, family, school, faith communities, and other influential parties compete for their fidelity.

- Formal essay: Writing a parable that provides a moral or lesson regarding people's loyalties to one another.

- Informal writing: Maintaining a "loyalty notebook" of news clippings, personal writing, and other explorations of loyalty in literature and life.

- Creative/multimedia project: Creating a board game that involves characters, pathways, and events studied in the unit. Players move toward a student-defined destination that in some way involves loyalty.

The Unit Outlines offered at www.coe.uga.edu/~smago/VirtualLibrary/ Unit_Outlines.htm provide many possibilities for orchestrating conceptual units into a curriculum of broad scope. We encourage readers to decide which are most appropriate for their students, school, and situation and arrange them into appropriate sequences and groupings.

Questions for Reflection

1. How can teaching the process of writing be accommodated within the other demands of teaching the English language arts curriculum?

2. How do you envision creating a curricular "spiral" so that students return to writing tasks routinely across the years of secondary education?

3. How might you revise Figure 9–1 in the sort of school you are teaching in?

4. What writing tasks do you think would be appropriate for the units in Figure 9–1? What tasks would be appropriate for any units that you would substitute for the ones currently listed?

5. How would you create a writing curriculum that is well-integrated with the literature curriculum?

6. How would you create a writing curriculum that is well-integrated with the language curriculum?

7. How would you create a writing curriculum that is responsive to the demands of testing mandates, but is also well-integrated with the literature and language curricula?

8. Would you emphasize any particular kinds of writing (literary analysis, extended definition, personal narratives, etc.) over others during the course of schooling? If so, why and how?

9. In planning a writing curriculum, how would you attend to the needs of English language learners and others whose cultural backgrounds do not prepare them well for the expectations of the curriculum?

10. How would you integrate technology into the overall writing curriculum?

References

Addington, A. H. 2001. "Talking About Literature in University Book Club and Seminar Settings." *Research in the Teaching of English* 36: 212–48.

American Psychological Association. 2001. *Publication Manual of the American Psychological Association,* 5th ed. Washington, DC: American Psychological Association.

Applebee, A. N. 1974. *Tradition and Reform in the Teaching of English: A History*. Urbana, IL: National Council of Teachers of English.

———. 1986. "Problems in Process Approaches: Toward a Reconceptualization of Process Instruction." In *The Teaching of Writing: 85th Yearbook of the National Society for the Study of Education,* edited by A. R. Petrosky and D. Bartholomae, 95–113. Chicago: University of Chicago Press.

———. 1993. *Literature in the Secondary School: Studies of Curriculum and Instruction in the United States*. Urbana, IL: National Council of Teachers of English.

———. 1996. *Curriculum as Conversation: Transforming Traditions of Teaching and Learning*. Chicago: University of Chicago Press.

Applebee, A. N., R. Burroughs, and A. Stevens. 2000. "Shaping Conversations: A Study of Devices That Create Continuity and Coherence in the High School Literature Curriculum." *Research in the Teaching of English* 34: 396–429.

Applebee, A. N., and J. A. Langer. 2006. *The State of Writing Instruction in America's Schools: What Existing Data Tell Us.* Albany, NY: National Writing Project, College Board, and Center on English Learning and Achievement. Retrieved December 16, 2008 from www.albany.edu/aire/news/State%20of%20Writing%20Instruction.pdf.

Bazerman, C., and J. Paradis, eds. 1991. *Textual Dynamics of the Professions: Historical and Contemporary Studies of Writing in Professional Communities.* Madison, WI: University of Wisconsin Press. Retrieved June 30, 2008 from www.wac.colostate.edu/books/textual_dynamics.

Beals, M. P. 1995. *Warriors Don't Cry.* New York: Washington Square Press.

Black, R. W. 2008. *Adolescents and Online Fan Fiction.* New York: Peter Lang.

Bruner, J. S. 1960. *The Process of Education.* Cambridge, MA: Harvard University Press.

———. 1986. *Actual Minds, Possible Worlds.* Cambridge, MA: Harvard University Press.

———. 1996. *The Culture of Education.* Cambridge, MA: Harvard University Press.

Burroughs, R. S., and P. Smagorinsky. 2009. "The Secondary English Curriculum and Adolescent Literacy." In *Handbook of Adolescent Literacy Research,* edited by L. Christenbury, R. Bomer, and P. Smagorinsky, 170–82. New York: Guilford.

Cole, M. 1996. *Cultural Psychology: A Once and Future Discipline.* Cambridge, MA: Harvard University Press.

———. 2005. "Cross-cultural and Historical Perspectives on the Developmental Consequences of Education." *Human Development* 48: 195–216.

Csikszentmihalyi, M. 1997. *Finding Flow: The Psychology of Engagement with Everyday Life.* New York: Basic Books.

Cuban, L. 1993. *How Teachers Taught: Constancy and Change in American Classrooms, 1890–1990.* New York: Teachers College Press.

Dale, H. 1997. *Co-authoring in the Classroom: Creating an Environment for Effective Collaboration.* Urbana, IL: National Council of Teachers of English.

Dell'Angelo, Tracy. 2004. "State Has a Strange Way with Words." *Chicago Tribune,* June 15, final ed., 1.

Gallas, K., and P. Smagorinsky. 2002. "Approaching Texts in School." *The Reading Teacher* 56 (1): 54–61.

Gevinson, S., D. Hammond, and P. Thompson. 2006. *Increase the Peace: A Program for Ending School Violence.* Portsmouth, NH: Heinemann.

Gibaldi, J. 2003. *MLA Handbook for Writers of Research Papers,* 6th ed. New York: Modern Language Association.

Graves, D. H. 1983. *Writing: Teachers and Children at Work.* Portsmouth, NH: Heinemann.

———.1989. *Investigate Nonfiction.* Portsmouth, NH: Heinemann.

———. 2003. *Writing: Teachers and Children at Work.* Portsmouth, NH: Heinemann.

Hillocks, G. 1964. *Concepts of Man: A Curriculum for Average Students.* Euclid, OH: Project English Demonstration Center (ED 017 492).

———. 1975. *Observing and Writing.* Urbana, IL: National Council of Teachers of English. Retrieved December 6, 2008 from www.coe.uga .edu/~smago/Books/Observing_and_Writing.pdf.

———. 1978. "A Multi-level Analysis of Teaching." Paper presented at the annual spring conference of the National Council of Teachers of English, Dallas, TX.

———. 1986a. *Research on Written Composition: New Directions for Teaching.* Urbana, IL: National Conference on Research in English and Educational Resources Information Center.

———. 1986b. "The Writer's Knowledge: Theory, Research, and Implications for Practice." In *The Teaching of Writing,* edited by A. R. Petrosky and E. Bartolamae, 71–94. Chicago: The University of Chicago Press, the National Society for the Study of Education.

———. 1995. *Teaching Writing as Reflective Practice.* New York: Teachers College Press.

———. 1999. *Ways of Thinking, Ways of Teaching.* New York: Teachers College Press.

———. 2002. *The Testing Trap: How State Writing Assessments Control Learning.* New York: Teachers College Press.

———. 2003. "Fighting Back: Assessing the Assessments." *English Journal* 92 (4): 63–70.

———. 2005. "The Focus on Form vs. Content in Teaching Writing." *Research in the Teaching of English* 40: 238–48.

———. 2006. *Narrative Writing: Learning a New Model for Teaching.* Portsmouth, NH: Heinemann.

Hillocks, G. Jr., E. Kahn, and L. Johannessen. 1983. "Teaching Defining Strategies as a Mode of Inquiry." *Research in the Teaching of English* 17: 275–84.

Hillocks, G., B. McCabe, and J. McCampbell. 1971. *The Dynamics of English Instruction, Grades 7–12.* New York: Random House. Retrieved August 4, 2006 from www.coe.uga.edu/~smago/Books/Dynamics/Dynamics_home .htm.

Hillocks, G., and J. F. McCampbell. 1965. *Talks on the Teaching of English.* Euclid, OH: Project English Demonstration Center and Case Western Reserve University.

Johannessen, L. R., E. Kahn, and C. C. Walter. 1982. *Designing and Sequencing Pre-writing Activities.* Urbana, IL: National Council of Teachers of English. Retrieved July 2, 2008 from www.coe.uga.edu/~smago/Books/Designing_ and_Sequencing.pdf.

———. 2009. *Writing About Literature, 2nd Edition, Revised and Updated.* Urbana, IL: National Council of Teachers of English.

Johnson, T. S., P. Smagorinsky, L. Thompson, and P. G. Fry. 2003. "Learning to Teach the Five-Paragraph Theme." *Research in the Teaching of English* 38: 136–76.

Kahn, E., C. C. Walter, and L. R. Johannessen. 1984. *Writing About Literature*. Urbana, IL: National Council of Teachers of English.

Lamm, K. 1998. *10,000 Ideas for Term Papers, Projects, Reports and Speeches*, 5th ed. New York: Macmillan.

Larson, R. 1988. "The High School 'Junior Theme' as an Adolescent Rite of Passage." *Journal of Youth and Adolescence* 17: 267–83.

Lee, C. D. 1993. *Signifying as a Scaffold for Literary Interpretation: The Pedagogical Implications of an African American Discourse Genre*. Urbana, IL: National Council of Teachers of English.

Marshall, J. D., P. Smagorinsky, and M. W. Smith. 1995. *The Language of Interpretation: Patterns of Discourse in Discussions of Literature*. NCTE Research Report No. 27. Urbana, IL: National Council of Teachers of English.

Marshall, J., and J. Smith. 1997. "Teaching as We're Taught: The University's Role in the Education of English Teachers." *English Education* 29: 246–68.

McCann, T. M. 1989. "Student Argumentative Writing Knowledge and Ability at Three Grade Levels. *Research in the Teaching of English* 23: 62–76.

McCann, T. M., L. R. Johannessen, E. Kahn, P. Smagorinsky, and M. W. Smith, eds. 2005. *Reflective Teaching, Reflective Learning: How to Develop Critically Engaged Readers, Writers, and Speakers*. Portsmouth, NH: Heinemann.

Nelson, J., and J. R. Hayes. 1988. *How the Writing Context Shapes College Students' Writing Strategies for Writing from Sources*. Center for the Study of Writing, Technical Report No. 16. Berkeley, CA and Pittsburgh, PA: University of California-Berkeley and Carnegie-Mellon University. ED 297374.

Nystrand, M. 1986. *The Structure of Written Communication*. Orlando, FL: Academic Press.

———. 1997. *Opening Dialogue: Understanding the Dynamics of Language and Learning in the English Classroom*. New York: Teachers College Press.

O'Donnell-Allen, C. 2006. *The Book Club Companion: Fostering Strategic Readers in the Secondary Classroom*. Portsmouth, NH: Heinemann.

Schneider, J. J. 2003. "Contexts, Genres, and Imagination: An Examination of the Idiosyncratic Writing Performances of Three Elementary Children Within Multiple Contexts of Writing Instruction." *Research in the Teaching of English* 37: 329–79.

Schultz, K. 2002. "Looking Across Space and Time: Reconceptualizing Literacy Learning In and Out of School." *Research in the Teaching of English* 36: 356–90.

Smagorinsky, P. 1991a. "The Writer's Knowledge and the Writing Process: A Protocol Analysis." *Research in the Teaching of English* 25: 339–64.

———. 1991b. "The Aware Audience: Role-Playing Peer Response Groups." *English Journal* 80 (5): 35–40.

———. 1999. "Time to Teach." *English Education* 32: 50–73.

———. 2008. *Teaching English by Design: How to Create and Carry Out Instructional Units*. Portsmouth, NH: Heinemann.

———. 2010. "Literacy Teaching and Learning in the Age of Accountability." In *Putting Writing Research into Practice: Applications for Teacher Professional Development*, edited by G. Troia, R. Shankland, and A. Heintz, 276–305. New York: Guilford.

Smagorinsky, P., N. Gibson, C. Moore, S. Bickmore, and L. Cook. 2004. "Praxis Shock: Making the Transition from a Student-Centered University Program to the Corporate Climate of Schools." *English Education* 36: 214–45.

Smagorinsky, P., T. McCann, and S. Kern. 1987. *Explorations: Introductory Activities for Literature and Composition, Grades 7–12*. Urbana, IL: National Council of Teachers of English. Retrieved December 8, 2008 from www .coe.uga.edu/~smago/Books/Explorations.pdf.

Smith, M. W. 1989. "Teaching the Interpretation of Irony in Poetry." *Research in the Teaching of English* 23: 254–72.

Smith, M. W., and J. D. Wilhelm. 2002. *"Reading Don't Fix No Chevys": Literacy in the Lives of Young Men*. Portsmouth, NH: Heinemann.

———. 2006. *Going with the Flow: How to Engage Boys (and Girls) in Their Literacy Learning*. Portsmouth, NH: Heinemann.

Toulmin, S. 1958. *The Uses of Argument*. New York: Cambridge University Press.

Toulmin, S. E., R. Rieke, and A. Janik. 1984. *An Introduction to Reasoning*, 2d ed. New York: Macmillan.

Tremmel, R. 2001. "Seeking a Balanced Discipline: Writing Teacher Education in First-Year Composition and English Education." *English Education* 34: 6–30.

Turabian, K. L. 2007. *A Manual for Writers of Research Papers, Theses, and Dissertations: Chicago Style for Students and Researchers*. Chicago: University of Chicago Press.

Wigginton, E., ed. 1972. *Foxfire Book: Hog Dressing, Log Cabin Building, Mountain Crafts and Foods, Planting by the Signs, Snake Lore, Hunting Tales, Faith Healing, Moonshining*. New York: Knopf.

Zeichner, K. M., and B. R. Tabachnik. 1981. "Are the Effects of Teacher Education 'Washed Out' by School Experience?" *Journal of Teacher Education* 32 (3): 7–11.

Author Biographies

Following his graduation as an English literature major from Kenyon College in 1974, **Peter Smagorinsky** completed the MAT program at the University of Chicago. He then taught English at Westmont, Barrington, and Oak Park/River Forest high schools from 1977–1990, coaching track and basketball as well. He received his doctorate from the University of Chicago in 1989 and has taught in the English Education programs at the University of Oklahoma (1990–1998) and the University of Georgia (1998–present). He has written and presented widely in state, national, and international publications and conferences on a variety of topics, including literacy across the high school curriculum, teaching and learning the English curriculum, the dynamics of small-group and whole-class discussions of literature, the composition of nonverbal texts across the high school curriculum, and the discourse of character education.

Elizabeth Kahn has taught English language arts for thirty-three years, currently at James B. Conant High School, where she is chair of the English department. She earned a BA in English from Wake Forest University and an MAT in English and a PhD in curriculum and instruction from the University of Chicago. She is coauthor of *Writing About Literature, 2nd Edition, Revised and*

Updated (NCTE 2009); *Talking in Class: Using Discussion to Enhance Teaching and Learning* (NCTE 2006); and *Designing and Sequencing Prewriting Activities* (NCTE 1982); and coeditor of *Reflective Teaching, Reflective Learning* (Heinemann 2005). She has published articles in *Research in the Teaching of English, English Journal, Journal of Educational Research, Clearing House, Curriculum Review,* and *Illinois English Bulletin.* She recently served on the NCTE Secondary Section Steering Committee, as president of the Illinois Association of Teachers of English, and is a National Board Certified Teacher.

Thomas M. McCann has taught English in a variety of schools, including eight years in an alternative school. He holds a BA from Northern Illinois University, an MA from Southern Illinois University, an MA from Saint Xavier University, and a PhD from the University of Chicago. He has taught and been an administrator at four high schools, at two colleges, and at three universities, where he worked with preservice and practicing teachers in graduate education programs. He is the coauthor of *Explorations: Introductory Activities for Literature and Composition, 7–12* (NCTE 1987); *In Case You Teach English: An Interactive Casebook for Prospective and Practicing Teachers* (Merrill/Prentice Hall 2002); *Talking in Class: Using Discussion to Enhance Teaching and Learning* (NCTE 2006); and *Supporting Beginning English Teachers* (NCTE 2005), which won NCTE's 2006 Richard A. Meade Award for Research in English Education. He is also the coeditor of *Reflective Teaching, Reflective Learning* (Heinemann 2005), and a column on mentoring for *English Journal.*

Larry R. Johannessen, 1947–2009

Larry Johannessen was born and raised in Denver, Colorado. When he went to register for classes in high school, his counselor slotted him into the vocational curriculum based on his working-class address. Dissatisfied with the assumptions behind this decision, Larry left high school before graduating and enlisted in the Marines, joining the same unit in which his father had served: B (Bravo) Company, 1st Reconnaissance Battalion, 1st Marine Division. This unit was later featured in the HBO series *Generation Kill,* which focused on the battalion's experiences in Iraq. Larry served two tours of duty in Vietnam, a country he had never heard of before enlisting. As a Marine, he was awarded the Presidential Unit Citation with one star, the National Defense Service Medal, the Vietnam Campaign Medal, the Vietnam Service Medal with three stars, the Good Conduct Medal, and the Rifle Marksman Badge (1964–68). He left the service with an honorable discharge in 1968 at the rank of sergeant.

Larry then earned his GED and entered Ohlone College, a two-year college in Fremont, California, from which he graduated with honors in 1973. He transferred to California State University Hayward (now East Bay), graduating *magna cum laude* in1975. In 1976, Larry earned his MAT in English Education from the University of Chicago, the program run by George Hillocks, Jr. At the University of Chicago, he met Elizabeth (Betsy) Kahn, whom he married. They had been married for twenty-seven years at the time of Larry's death.

Larry taught high school English at Lyons Township High School in LaGrange, Illinois, from 1976 to 1989. He began working on his doctoral studies in 1983 at the University of Chicago, again under the mentorship of George Hillocks. He completed his degree in 1997. While a doctoral student, he began teaching at universities, including St. Xavier University in Chicago; Benedictine University in Lisle, Illinois; and Barat College in Lake Forest, Illinois. In 2001 he became a professor of English at Northern Illinois University. During his career at NIU, he served as director of undergraduate studies.

Larry was a prolific author and presenter. His writing was published in a variety of journals, including *English Journal*, *Clearing House*, *Research in the Teaching of English*, and *Social Education*. He was also the author, coauthor, or coeditor of nine books published by Heinemann, NCTE, and Merrill, plus two textbooks on vocabulary study for Kendall/Hunt. Larry's work fell into three general areas: teaching the literature of the Vietnam War, designing instruction using a structured process approach, and studying the experiences of beginning English teachers. Many of these publications were coauthored with his wife, Elizabeth Kahn, and his close friend Tom McCann.

Larry's academic career earned him a number of awards. From NCTE he won the 2006 Richard A. Meade Award presented annually to recognize published research that investigates English/Language Arts teacher development at any educational level, of any scope, and in any setting. He was the recipient of the 2003 Illinois Association for Supervision and Curriculum Development Winn Research Award. Northern Illinois University gave him the 2007 NIU Ally Award, presented to individuals who have done something positive for the lesbian, gay, bisexual, transgender community at NIU, and also presented him with the College of Liberal Arts and Sciences 2005–06 Long-Term Merit/Critical Retention Award. He has been listed in a number of biographical volumes, including *Who's Who Among America's Teachers*, *Who's Who in American Education, Men of Achievement*, and the *Dictionary of International Biography*. In 1973 he received the Outstanding Ohlone College English Student Award, and in 1990 was honored with an Ohlone College Outstanding Alumnus Award. The Illinois Institute of Technology honored him with a Distinguished High School Teachers of the Chicago Area Award in 1981.

Larry died on Tuesday, April 21, 2009, at Rush Medical Center in Chicago of complications related to Myelodysplastic Syndrome, possibly resulting from his exposure to Agent Orange, the defoliant used in Vietnam during his tours of duty. Larry was a beloved husband, friend, colleague, teacher, and mentor. We, and so many who crossed his path during his remarkable life, will miss him dearly.

Index